Customize the Brand

Make it more desirable – and profitable

Torsten H Nilson

JOHN WILEY & SONS, LTD

Published in 2003 by   John Wiley & Sons Ltd, The Atrium, Southern Gate, Chichester,
West Sussex PO19 8SQ, England

Telephone (+44) 1243 779777

Email (for orders and customer service enquiries): cs-books@wiley.co.uk
Visit our Home Page on www.wileyeurope.com or www.wiley.com

This publication is designed to provide accurate and authoritative information in regard
to the subject matter covered. It is sold on the understanding that the Publisher is not
engaged in rendering professional services. If professional advice or other expert
assistance is required, the services of a competent professional should be sought.

Other Wiley Editorial Offices

John Wiley & Sons, Inc., 111 River Street, Hoboken, NJ 07030, USA

Jossey-Bass, 989 Market Street, San Francisco, CA 94103-1741, USA

Wiley-VCH Verlag GmbH, Boschstr. 12, D-69469 Weinheim, Germany

John Wiley & Sons Australia, Ltd, 33 Park Road, Milton, Queensland 4064, Australia

John Wiley & Sons (Asia) Pte, Ltd, 2 Clementi Loop #02-01, Jin Xing Distripark,
Singapore 129809

John Wiley & Sons Canada Ltd, 22 Worcester Road, Etobicoke, Ontario M9W 1L1,
Canada

British Library Cataloguing in Publication Data
A catalogue record for this book is available from the British Library

ISBN 0–470–84822–7

Project management by Originator, Gt Yarmouth, Norfolk (typeset in 11/13pt Palatino)
Printed and bound in Great Britain by T.J. International Ltd, Padstow, Cornwall.
This book is printed on acid-free paper responsibly manufactured from sustainable
forestry, in which at least two trees are planted for each one used for paper production.

Contents

Preface

Average marketing delivers average results. Average marketing builds average brands. Working with averages is just no fun.

To compromise is to lose the edge. Mass-marketing methods can only ever deliver a compromise, as it has to be based on the common denominator. I personally do not mind compromising with people I know, and many times I have wished more people around the world would be more willing to compromise. However, to deliver a brand promise based on a compromise is not a good way to start the day.

Focus is king – in particular in brand marketing. So much marketing activity is wasted because it is not relevant to the audience. With 32,000 brands advertised in the UK alone and 3,000 commercial messages per day, any message, any activity, any product or service must fight hard to get a hearing – to be relevant, to be different. Focus is what it takes.

To customize the brand is to do away with averages and compromises. It allows you to focus the marketing activities, to deliver relevant, appealing and differentiating brand propositions. And, all it takes is a different perspective that we call 'customized branding'.

To *Customize the Brand* means that you develop a brand people actually want to buy, not just buying it because nothing else is available or the salesperson seems to be a nice guy. Your brand will develop into something truly desirable, and, importantly, something that is more desirable than what the competition can offer.

To customize the brand will deliver more money to the company. Why? Because what is being sold will be worth more to the customer. It will be more relevant and more useful. It will appeal to the senses in a way that an ordinary brand can't. That is what it takes to build loyalty, and with greater loyalty comes sustainable profits.

The customized branding concept has grown out of the work we have done in The Quant. Marketing Company – the 'data-driven brand marketing' consultancy I run with my business partner and co-owner Nigel Gatehouse. We have from our start, two years ago, been fascinated by the opportunity to build stronger brands by using customer data to enhance customer understanding, and then develop segmented brand propositions to deliver a superior brand experience. This book explains why you should start thinking about this *now* and will of course also explain how to do it.

Just as in my previous books I have mixed practical examples with conclusions, advice and the odd theory. All is based on my observations of what companies do. In some cases I have used material in the public domain, sometimes not. In some cases I have had to avoid mentioning the name of the brand and/or company of the example for confidentiality reasons although rest assured that each example is genuine.

Most of these examples do refer to consumer products or services. The reason is that, in general, consumer goods are better known, as we are all consumers and can relate to consumer issues. This does not mean that this is a book just about consumer goods. Far from it. Business-to-business companies have actually in many cases much greater opportunities to apply the principles of the book successfully.

Please note a semantic issue. I have in many cases used the term 'product' in a very generic sense covering all kinds of products and services, and combinations of the two. On occasion I have expressed what is being sold as 'product and/or service' or 'product/service package', but in many cases, to avoid repetitiveness, I have just written 'product'.

Finally, a disclaimer: This is not a book about basic branding. If you just want to know how to build a brand, I suggest you read my previous book *Competitive Branding* (John Wiley & Sons, 1998).

In this book I have assumed that the reader is familiar with the basic branding concept. However, I may still have repeated some basic truths. This is either because I felt it is necessary to establish the context or that I simply felt it appropriate. If in this way I have bored someone, I humbly apologize.

I have enjoyed writing this book. I do hope you will enjoy reading it and that it will help you to develop a successful customized branding strategy. If you have any comments regarding the book, don't hesitate to email me on either thnilson@aol.com or torsten.nilson@quantmarketing.com.

Torsten H Nilson
Tunbridge Wells, Kent, UK
October 2002

Acknowledgements

I would like to thank all those who have made this book possible. I am extremely grateful to all my colleagues and clients who over the years – knowingly and unknowingly – have contributed with information, views and ideas.

A particular and sincere thank you is extended to my business partner in The Quant. Marketing Company, Nigel Gatehouse for his advice, ideas and encouragement, all of fundamental importance to the book. Nigel's contributions have been particularly useful in the areas of customer data and segmentation.

The examples in the book come from a variety of sources. Some come from my consultancy and line management experience while others are based on what friends and colleagues have told me. Many have their origins in newspapers, magazines and books. In particular I would like to mention *The Economist*, *Financial Times*, *Forbes* magazine, *Harvard Business Review*, the Swedish *Veckans Affärer*, the UK trade journals *Marketing*, *Marketing Week* and *The Grocer*.

I would also like to thank Claire Plimmer and the team at John Wiley & Sons for their positive help and support.

Finally a big thank you to my wife Annika for doing all the things I should have done if I had not decided to write this book.

Introduction

Individuals make all purchasing decisions. Whether it is a 20-year-old unemployed in a poor urban area looking for a cheap meal, a wealthy housewife in the city centre buying a new handbag, the pensioner in a small town splashing out on a box of chocolates, or the buyer of cable for a building company, a marketing director buying advertising space, a chief executive negotiating to buy a manufacturing plant, they are all decisions made by individuals either on their own or as part of a group.

Yet, almost all brand marketing assumes that we are all the same, that we are part of a target group definition. If the definition is tightly made, as it should be, most probably only a minority of the actual customers will be part of it. If it is not made that way and a wide definition such as 'housewives 25–50 years old and ABC1 social class' is used, it is not a homogeneous group and thus the message, product or delivery system will not be all that appropriate to all that many.

The reality is that the closer we get to each individual, the more we understand about the individual and his/her circumstances, the better we can communicate, the better we can provide and offer something that is truly relevant and different. We can also offer a price that is optimal from the perspective of the individual transaction and it can all be delivered the way the customer wants.

That is one part of the rationale for customized branding. The other part has its origin in pure branding theory and is that the brand is a reflection of what happens in the minds of the customers.

2   Customize the Brand

'Brands' and 'branding' are among the most overused and mishandled words in the marketing vocabulary. 'Branding' is not designing a new logo, nor introducing a new visual identity – contrary to articles in the marketing press. A 'brand' is a symbol of a product (Coca-Cola), service (Eurostar trains), company (Campari) or even an individual (Michael Jordan) to identify what it is. In doing that it encapsulates the accumulated reputation of that particular 'unit'. That reputation can be an effect of personal experiences, brand owner communication, what friends, relatives and others have said, what has been written and said about it in various media, etc.

The perception of a brand is formed in the minds of human beings, the audience. It is not formed behind a desk or in a conference room. All the brand owner can do is to work as hard as possible to manage all the channels to the individual so that the perception in the mind of the individual matches the one on the paper in front of the marketing director, and vice versa.

To be able to achieve this match between desired perception and reality, the marketing director does need that piece of paper with the key elements of the brand written down and well defined. Only by having the various elements defined, will it be possible to orchestrate the activities of the company so that the match in perceptions is achieved.

Bringing the two parts together is what building a customized brand is all about. By getting close to the individual, the brand becomes more relevant. By knowing more, the brand can be better defined. By delivering products and services with real benefit, the brand gets stronger. By communicating in an appealing and exciting way, the brand is strengthened. By treating people like individuals rather than an average mass of people who may or may not have a lot in common, the branding process becomes immensely more effective, generating more sales, more customer satisfaction and consequently more profits, and it is sustainable profits because they come from a brand that is truly relevant and one that has the potential to stay relevant over time and earn the customers' loyalty.

1
The customized brand – introducing the concept

SOME BACKGROUND

Not so long ago everything was customized. The product you bought was made especially for you by people who knew who you were and who personally understood your needs and wants. The seller knew a lot about the customer, the customer most of the time knew a lot about the seller. The customer still knows a lot about the seller, some of it positive, some negative. He or she will have had some personal experience or, if not, a friend or colleague may have. There may have been some advertising or something may have come through the post. The experience may have been a positive – 'I like that advertisement' – or negative – 'What a rude shop assistant'. With more communication, more access to information, the customer will gain more and more knowledge about his or her supplier.

On the other hand, in most cases, the seller rarely knows a lot about the customer. Who he or she or they really are? What do they really want? What kind of product? What kind of service? More features or less? Unless there is a personal contact, the actual knowledge and information used is minimal. Sales records, market research data and qualitative feedback from the company front line is the maximum amount of information in the vast majority of companies – and most of it is 'faceless', based on limited data aggregated up to an 'average'.

4   Customize the Brand

So, while the customer is increasing his or her knowledge all the time and sometimes even takes charge and turns the selling process into a buying process via Internet buying clubs or electronic marketplaces, the people doing the selling are still operating the same old way – perhaps using new tools such as the Web, but applying the same approach built around an average view of the world.

With customized branding this will change. And the companies and brand managements that don't will be followers in the market, not leaders. Not a good thing as market leaders tend to be more profitable and longer lasting than the followers.

Buyers have been improving their knowledge of the sellers while the sellers have made little progress in learning more about the buyers. Time for a change!

THE CUSTOMIZED BRAND

A customized brand is **a brand with a proposition that is customized to the individual's particular circumstances, requirements, needs and desires**.

To customize a brand is to **adapt the brand's proposition and the brand platform to each individual in the target market without losing the identity and profile of the brand**.

A customized brand delivers to each customer an individualized total brand experience.

By customizing the brand it is possible to define and deliver a brand proposition that is designed for and delivered to each individual customer in such a way that it is perceived to be made 'just for me'. Such a brand will be much more appealing and relevant than competitive mass-market offerings. It will also be better differentiated as it will appear in a much more well-defined marketplace – a market of one.

Taking charge of the branding process in this way has a number of implications. Most of them will be covered in the different chapters of this book. By taking the initiative the brand owners will start to recover any ground lost and take charge of the commercial process. By understanding what each customer wants, it is possible to design and deliver solutions that are superior to what the competition can do, and what the customer expects.

Customers are more or less committed to the brand they buy. Many buy a particular product as a matter of routine and lack of choice – in effect they are not committed at all. Even more customers buy from a repertoire of brands, on each occasion choosing almost randomly or on the basis of the influence of special offers – committed to brand*s*, rather than a brand. A strong brand will, finally, have a core of dedicated, committed customers – usually representing a minority of the total customer universe.

By applying the principles of customizing a brand, the level of commitment will increase as the brand proposition will be more relevant. But, the commitment is not 'for free', it requires a full adaptation of the total marketing mix, from product development and distribution to promotion and advertising.

If, on the other hand, a brand owner continues with a traditional mass-market approach, even spiced up by Internet solutions and CRM systems, the customers will increasingly continue to take charge. The company will in the end become a subcontractor of their wishes and be subject to a marketplace where every product and service is commoditized and all sales are done on the basis of lowest price. For most companies that is not a bright future.

Very few concepts are totally new, and neither is customized branding. Some companies already now apply and use some or even several of the elements of building a customized brand. This is fortunate as otherwise (a) the book would not have any examples and (b) it would be impossible to conclude that this is a very effective way to run a business. However, utterly few take a total view and actually apply all the elements systematically. It is a piecemeal approach, in most cases driven by opportunities rather than strategy. The exception being certain industries where mass-market thinking never has entered the office, such as big project consulting, bespoke furniture makers and private banking for the super-rich.

Customized branding was until fairly recently not a practical proposition for many companies and brands. Customer information was usually not available, and, if it was, it was not accessible in a practical way. The knowledge to structure data and information was not developed and a wide spectrum of communication channels was not developed, so it was not possible to communicate in a specific way. All that is now available and is waiting for marketing executives to make full use of it.

Just do it!

MORE REASONS

An important side effect of working within a framework of customized branding is that much more information about the customers will become available. How to use this for customized branding will be covered later, but all marketing decisions will benefit.

Decisions can be made against a background of much better information which should lead to better decisions and more successful marketing, even if the company is not able to implement all aspects of a customized brand building process.

A customized branding approach is a tremendous opportunity to build a sustainable business. As I will show in this book, it makes it possible to create an offer, which can generate genuine desire to buy on the part of the customers while ensuring that the supplier gets sustainable profits. Previously only an artisan could do this because it required individual, personal attention. It was not an approach that was cost-competitive in the modern world. Now this has changed, as it is possible to customize every element of the brand building process. Very few companies have woken up to this fact so the first to take a comprehensive approach will be long-term winners and build a competitive advantage.

More information – better decisions. With a customized brand better performance and sustainable profits.

ISN'T CUSTOMIZED BRANDING JUST THE SAME AS THE OLD ONE-TO-ONE MARKETING AND CRM CONCEPTS?

The answer to this question is of course *no*. It is however a relevant question in that both these concepts are related to the thinking behind customized branding and can well be a part of a customized brand plan.

One-to-one marketing is essentially a method to sell more by more persuasive communication. The method to make it more convincing is to individualize the message from the supplier for each possible target. In its simplest form it is nothing more than personally addressed direct mail; in its more advanced form, the message is adapted to suit the recipient's personal circumstances.

The difference between building a customized brand and one-to-one marketing is the scope of the process. Building a brand is much more than communication and selling, it is about developing a proposition, it is adapting the offer, it is using customer knowledge not only to bring about better communication but to offer a more attractive and relevant product.

One-to-one marketing is like the old corner shop, the range is fixed but the shop owner knows his customers so he can adapt the presentation to each individual's circumstances. Customized branding is like the artisan. He not only knows what the customer wants and the customer's circumstances, he understands the context and his own skills so that he can offer something special and unexpected that is better than what the customer expected. The range is not fixed as in the grocery store, the range can be modified and adapted to suit the special circumstances of the customer.

CRM, customer relationship management, is one of the most misused terms in business. It is often used to describe a computer system that logs all customer interfaces and provides a single customer view that each person in the company can use in his or her relations with the customer. If it is true to the concept, it should also provide a channel for the customer's feedback to filter back into the company. CRM is a way to manage customer relations, a consequence of a customer contact strategy.

CRM is not an alternative to building a customized brand but a possible implementation tool. If applied as a way of thinking, it can be most useful. If it is considered equal to a computerized customer contact system, it is a highly doubtful approach unless the customer and contact strategy has first been defined in a solid way following on from establishing a customized brand strategy.

In reality most investments in CRM 'systems' have failed. According to an article in *Harvard Business Review*, CRM ranks among the bottom three for satisfaction in the league table of management techniques and one in five executives reported that CRM not only has failed to deliver any benefits but actually damaged customer relationships.

> **One-to-one marketing and CRM can be useful tools for implementing a customized brand strategy. It is not a substitute.**

SUCCESS, PERFORMANCE, EVEN EXCEPTIONAL DESIRE

Some brands already today are symbols of desire. Robberies carried out by teenagers to get their new Nike trainers a couple of years ago were in one sense the ultimate symbol of desire. A Mercedes-Benz (as immortalized by Janis Joplin in the song *Oh, Lord Won't You Buy Me A Mercedes-Benz*), a Barbour coat, a Prada handbag or the latest version of Sony's Playstation are for different categories brands to long for. These brands deliver more than just functional benefits, be it status, 'street-cred', a sense of tradition or any other intangible brand value. The sustainable desirable brand delivers both superior functional and emotional brand values.

Truly desirable brands are very few and the desire is often restricted to a few segments of the market. While many buy Nikes, few desire them. Not everyone desires a Mercedes-Benz, nor a Prada handbag or Barbour coat. A Playstation is highly desirable for some but the longer it is on the market, the less desirable it becomes. While it is difficult to achieve and maintain the exceptional status of the brands mentioned above, it is perfectly possible to lift any brand above the average level of mediocrity where many mass-market brands currently float, to a successful brand with a level of desire which will enable the brand to prosper in the longer term and become a generator of company profits for years to come.

The clue to such a successful brand is simply to make the brand more relevant, and the way to do that is to customize the brand proposition so that each customer deep down feels that 'this company understands me' and 'they sure make something I want to have'.

Customizing the brand proposition will make the brand totally relevant for each individual customer

2

From the mark of a maker to a symbol of desire, and from mass-market to customization twice over

There is a reason for everything and by understanding at least some of the background to a concept, it becomes much easier to grasp and to adapt to our own circumstances. The purpose of this chapter is to give some of that background.

Brands are not a recent invention, nor a marketing luxury. They are as old as our writing and as necessary as any other element of a company's, or individual's, commercial activities.

Originally a brand was just the mark of a maker. To identify who had made a product, you 'branded' the goods with your name. The word 'brand' itself comes from the Scandinavian word for 'fire' (= *brand*) and 'branding' is literally to mark something with fire, just like they used to do with cattle in the Wild West.

Whether you were Antonio Stradivari of Cremona making the best violins (the Stradivarius) the world has seen or Henry Ford making the cheapest cars the world had ever seen, the brand was the name of the maker.

THE FIRST MASS-MARKET BRANDS

The first brands were very much made for everyone, or at least that is what we assume, as we do not really know. The first brands were Egyptian, originating from around 3200 BC, and were found next to a bale of cloth and a jug which had contained wine. The hieroglyphs, which constituted the brand name, described where the goods came from and, as far as we can understand, it was very much standard cloth and wine. These hieroglyphs were not only the first brands, but also constituted the first writing ever found. In other words, branding is as old as our writing. Far from an invention of the 19th or 20th centuries.

The first brands were for the mass-market, 5,000 years ago.

> Mass-marketing

THE FIRST CUSTOMIZED BRANDS

As business developed through the ages, craftsmen and traders became increasingly skilled in adapting to their markets, and their goods became increasingly customized. Great brands like Leonardo da Vinci (anything creative), Rembrandt (paintings), Chippendale (furniture) and the above-mentioned Stradivari produced products to order. They knew the customer, knew what he wanted (not many female customers in those days) and knew what the customer was prepared to pay (the Medici family in Italy surely paid more for a painting than a Dutch burgher a couple of hundred years later). By customizing the product, the supplier got a more satisfied customer because he got what he wanted, not a standard product. The seller could also charge more because the customer was more satisfied. The producer customized because it made financial sense as the cost for customization was less than the additional revenue generated by the sale.

Then they realized that much more could be charged for a customized brand

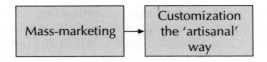

MASS-MARKETING FOR THE MASSES

However, the world of the artisan was shattered in the 19th century. Industrialization, and all that followed with this phenomenon, meant that mass-production with its cost-effectiveness took over and the artisan was left with the niche market of individually crafted pieces for the select few.

To make mass-production viable you needed transport, provided by trains and ships, and mass-marketing. Messrs Procter, Gamble, Lever, Edison, Heinz, Nestlé, Ford and many others developed mass-marketing through trial and error and in the process founded modern branding.

The aim was first to identify the maker – as always – but they soon realized that more was possible, and needed. If you are making soap and sending it across a continent you need to provide not only the guarantee of a name but also information. What is so good about this product? Why should anyone buy it? From tangible benefits such as standardized quality to intangible benefits such as feelings of 'doing the right thing', 'if I use this soap I will look beautiful' or 'as I am using the same soap as famous people, I will also look like the famous people'.

Mass-marketing was back in fashion, not least because of the economies of scale. With big sales you could develop much more aggressive advertising, product development and sales. The traditionalist artisans soon disappeared from the mainstream.

Mass-marketing brought branded goods to the masses

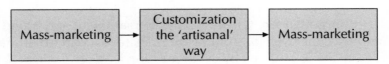

CUSTOMIZING FOR THE MASS-MARKET

We have now come full circle second time around. The cost penalties traditionally linked to customization no longer apply. With the right thinking, methods, mechanics and implementation, it is possible to provide that feeling of individuality, providing something that is seen as being made 'especially for me or us', while maintaining economies of scale. While the premium price a company will be able to charge will be considerably less than in the 16th and 17th centuries, the customized business with or without a premium price will be much more sustainable than if applying average mass-marketing. It will not be necessary to reduce the prices down to the lowest common denominator to get a sale and, above all, the customers will really like to buy the brand.

In the past the only way of achieving a similar level of customized product was to adapt a niche strategy. Once a company had realized it could not serve the whole market with 'one size fits all', the management had to identify the segment or niche, consisting of those customers 'fitting the one size' and then strive to dominate that niche by providing the 'one size' in a way which was superior to what all other suppliers could do.

With customized branding there is not the need to make that compromise – that is, losing the benefits of a large brand such as economies of scale in strategy, production and marketing – to be able to compete effectively. It is still possible to be a mass-market brand but to do it in a way which means that the customer view is one of a supplier providing exactly what he or she wants while at the same time have all the benefits of a big brand. The financial benefits of a big brand (= profits) are combined with customization (leading to superior performance and sustainability) to provide the best of both worlds.

It is now possible to customize and still serve the mass-market.

An often-forgotten fact when it comes to marketing and branding is that we can learn a lot from history. There is a pattern of mass-marketing being replaced by customization as soon as the benefits

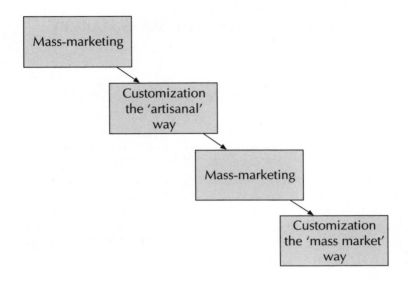

of customization outweigh any cost penalty created by achieving an individualized product or service. The customer of today, and tomorrow, is not prepared to buy 'one size fits all' any more unless it is cheaper, and noticeably cheaper. Those companies that first understand that to build a sustainable business it is necessary to individualize and customize, and that it is possible to do so while remaining cost-competitive, will win. Not only in the marketplace but also in the hearts and minds of the customers.

People always prefer a customized brand to a standardized one but only if it can be delivered at a price close to that of a mass-marketed brand.

3
Leading the way

One of the fundamental rules of marketing is that if you want to be a leader in the market, you have to act as a leader. By leading the way you keep the initiative, you stay ahead of competitors and you avoid falling into the copycat position which is, in most cases, a less good and less profitable position. This chapter explores some key concepts to help brands stay ahead of competition.

LEAD THE MARKET AND OTHER FUNDAMENTALS

To be able to *lead the market* and act as a leader it is necessary to lead the customers. If the company, as per the old-fashioned part of marketing theory, only listens to the customers and then delivers what the customer is asking for, the brand will inevitably, sooner or later, be overtaken in the market. The reason is that unless there is a turnaround time of zero (i.e. it is possible to deliver what is asked for immediately), the company will fall behind. By the time the company has developed, produced and delivered what the customers said they wanted, they may well have changed their minds and/or a competitor may have already launched something into the marketplace fulfilling the need. In addition it is impossible for a customer to know what a supplier can deliver. Simply to follow the customers is to abdicate the management of the company and the brand to the customers – and abdicating responsibility is rarely a way to build a strong brand and business.

This does not mean avoiding listening to the customers. The reverse is true. It is crucial to understand different customers fully. It is actually impossible to build a strong brand, and in particular a strong customized brand, without having a thorough understanding of the customer. But it is only the beginning. From its understanding of the customer, the company must build its proposition, develop its products, build its brand and deliver what will take the market forward.

Being number one in the minds of the customers is another essential ingredient in building a successful brand business. The reasoning behind this statement is very well described by the creator of the concept, Jack Trout, in several of his books, from *Positioning – The Battle for Your Mind* (with Al Ries) to *Differentiate or Die*.

The business realities are that there are considerable benefits in being considered first in a category. If a brand is the number one when it comes to safe cars (Volvo in most markets), everybody intending to buy a safe car will consider that brand. They may not buy, but they will consider it. That is a much better position than being second in a category as then the brand will only be considered once all potential customers have rejected number one. For a brand to be number one it needs to be differentiated from others in the sector. This is a crucial part of developing the brand.

In a survey published in *McKinsey Quarterly* it takes 107,000 prospects to generate 100,000 sales of Mercedes-Benz cars. For the brand Isuzu it takes 1,300,000 prospects to generate sales of 100,000 cars. To be the preferred choice, first in mind, rather than a car that is considered as a second or third alternative, has some significant advantages from a sales and profit point of view. The more effective the conversion rate, the more effective the sales process and, everything else being equal, the more profitable the brand will be.

A company executive who has a target of being less than number one should not, in my view, be in business – and certainly not in marketing. If the brand already is a number one, the task is to consolidate the position and make sure it is number one in all segments. If not number one, devise and implement a plan to get to the number one position, either by redefining the category or toppling the current number one. Customized branding could well be the strategy to achieve this objective.

As will be described in greater detail in Chapter 4, the world is getting increasingly complex, and corporate life is no exception. To be successful in such an environment, in particular when it comes to branding, it is necessary to *simplify and focus*. It is impossible to go to great depths on each and every issue. It is necessary to simplify the issues, make them easy to grasp so that it is possible to focus on what is really important. The paradox of the statement is that it does require a fair amount of work and experience to be able to simplify the right way and focus on the right issues. It is, however, essential. It is essential from a management point of view and it is also essential for the customers. Unless the message, in whatever form, is focused and easy to understand, it will not cut through the noise level of today's marketplace, whatever the market sector and whatever the country.

It may seem a truism to state that it is essential to be *relevant*. However, to be totally relevant is not that easy. It requires thorough customer understanding to be able to know what could be relevant and then creativity and marketing skill to convert the customer understanding to a product and/or service that is truly relevant and to communicate it in a way which strikes a chord with the audience.

The final point of these marketing fundamentals is that for any successful business you have to deliver to such a degree that you *ensure repeat purchase*. If not, the company will sooner or later run out of customers. There are of course products and services you do not buy very often, examples being private matters like wedding or funeral services or financial commitments such as a pension plan; but also in these situations it is essential to deliver to the level of ensuring a repeat purchase. The individual may not buy again but the individual's friends or relatives may well – and will ask a previous customer for advice. There is a multitude of studies proving and illustrating that if the number of loyal customers goes up so will profits. And common sense supports the evidence. It is more expensive to recruit a new customer than getting a repeat from an existing one, so repeat business must be more profitable.

These five marketing fundamentals are essential for any business in any circumstance. They are, though, particularly relevant in the context of developing a customized brand:

- *Lead the market* – customized branding is a new concept. The first to apply the principles in each sector will be a leader. Tesco is the most successful grocery retailer in the UK. One reason is that it is further down the road to customized branding than its competitors.
- *Be number one* – to be number one is important, to be number one in the mind of each customer is even more important. Customizing the brand will help to achieve this.
- *Simplify and focus* – customized branding does in one sense make the world even more confused and over-communicated because the message is adapted to suit each customer category. The way to cope is to simplify and focus.
- *Be relevant* – the purpose of having a customized brand is to be more relevant than the competition.
- *Ensure repeat purchases* – this goal for a successful business is the reward for a well-developed brand proposition. The customized brand will be in a stronger position than a traditional mass-market brand to deliver a product or service that will be so appreciated that there is no doubt as to whether a repeat purchase will take place or not.

THE FOUR STAGES TO ACHIEVING TOTAL RELEVANCE

Companies and brands are at different levels on the road to total relevance.

At the first level, the most basic one, the ambition is to do whatever is done 'better'. This approach is not to be ignored. It is a very important ambition for any company wanting to survive, as if you do not have it you will be overtaken and disappear from the market very soon. (The key processes to becoming a 'better' brand is described in my book *Value-added Marketing* published in 1992 by McGraw-Hill.)

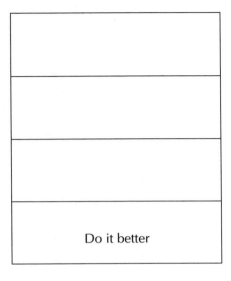

Although important, it is not enough to say: 'We do what everyone else is doing – but we do it better!' This is far too bland. There is no profile, no differentiation, no reason to buy apart from 'we are better'. Not enough for a strong brand.

The second stage is to develop different products or services for different categories. Many companies have been successful with this strategy but usually only for a while. The Japanese boom in the 1970s was built on this strategy. 'We have any version of vehicle or consumer electronics you like. And we may even throw in a couple of extra features for free as a bonus.'

However, we now know that the strategy ran out of steam after some 10 years. Many FMCG (fast-moving consumer goods) companies have adapted a similar strategy, providing a wide range of goods so that there is bound to be something for everyone. Again, in the face of more distinct competition it has become increasingly difficult to just deliver a multitude of products and services and then let the potential customer pick and choose. In more recent times the same strategy has been used in the IT sector with similarly disappointing results.

The reason for the lack of long-term success is that once the novelty and first mover advantage has disappeared and all other companies also offer a wide range, there is no longer a reason to

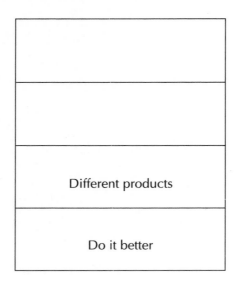

choose a particular brand. The brands, such as Nissan or Panasonic, are left with no profile and no point of difference and the customers can't take in the wide choice as it disappears, 'drowns', in our world of communication overflow. The strategy works as an interim one, during that short period when choice alone is a basis for differentiation, but for the longer term the result is lack of success.

The third stage is to differentiate the brand. By being different to competition in a relevant way, the future of a brand is on a sound and solid foundation. A strong differentiation is built on a distinct positioning and strong brand values.

In most markets up until now, this has been enough. By differentiating the brand and the offer, there is a reason for customers to choose your brand instead of someone else's. Not many companies and brands have achieved a differentiating position. The reality is, unfortunately for most companies, that there is less differentiation. In a survey published in *Harvard Business Review* by Kevin Clancy and Jack Trout, consumers stated that among 46 categories only 2 were rated as being increasingly distinct and there was no change in 4, but in 40 categories brands in the same category were converging and becoming less distinct.

The fourth and last stage to a totally relevant offer is to base

Differentiate the brand
Different products
Do it better

your brand development on all the above *plus* an ability to provide something that is perceived as 'especially for me'. By understanding what each part of the target audience actually wants, it is possible to develop, deliver and communicate totally appropriate products and services and thus build a totally

Customize the brand
Differentiate the brand
Different products
Do it better

relevant brand that is differentiated not only on total market level but in the minds of each current and potential customer.

There are three elements to achieving this. First, a thorough understanding of the target audience so that each category's needs, wants and desires can be defined. Second, a differentiating brand platform as per Stage 3, a variety of products and services as per Stage 2 and a superior product or service as per Stage 1. Third, an ability to develop, deliver and communicate a customized brand proposition.

The four stages are (1) superior delivery, (2) offer choice, (3) differentiate from competition and (4) customize the brand proposition.

INTRODUCING THE THREE BUILDING BLOCKS TO CUSTOMIZED BRANDING

The steps to creating a customized brand are built around three building blocks:

1 Understand the target audience.
2 Develop and deliver a customized product and/or service.
3 Communicate with the target audience in an individual-centred way.

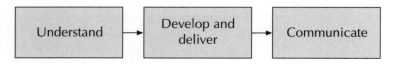

Understanding the target audience is crucial to the success of any marketing strategy but more so with customized branding as it is not only a question of generating enough understanding to develop one solution. The task is to achieve such a thorough customer understanding that it will be possible to develop and adapt the brand proposition to the many different parts of the target audience.

There is a difference in concept and methodology between

understanding your customers and understanding the target audience. For some companies it is enough to understand the customers, for others the scope is wider. Regardless, it makes sense, unless you are new on the market, to start by trying to understand your current customers. This is important in order to ensure repeat purchases, the core of the business. It is also important to be able to understand the total target audience, as by understanding the current customers, clues can be found to make it easier to spot possible future customers. The technique is sometimes referred to as 'searching for twins' (i.e. looking for potential customers who are 'like a twin' to an existing customer).

There are many different ways of achieving customer understanding. The simplest one is to talk to as many as possible. Retailing is an industry highly dependent on consumer satisfaction. Almost all successful retailers spend considerable time at the front line talking to customers. Retail legends such as John Sainsbury (Sainsbury's), Ian MacLaurin (Tesco) as well as Wal-Mart's Sam Walton and IKEA founder Ingvar Kamprad spent, or in Kamprad's case still spend despite being 70+, considerable time in talking face-to-face with customers.

Michael Dell of Dell Computers has stated that the most valuable customers to Dell are not the customers who spend the most but those who challenge the Dell company the most by questioning Dell's products and services.

At the other end of the customer understanding spectrum is using sophisticated technology to process customer data to understand why people do what they do. One of the best examples of this in the world is Tesco, the UK retailer. By using customer data generated through the Tesco Clubcard (a so-called loyalty card), Tesco understands its customers better than most, if not all, other retailers. This has provided Tesco with a significant competitive advantage. But, first, having lots of customer data is not a reason for not talking to customers. Second, it is not enough to understand your customers, you have to strive toward understanding them better than anyone else. That is the only way to maintain the competitive advantage.

To *develop and deliver* a customized product or service was until recently the prerogative of the artisan, as explained earlier. Mass-production did not allow individual attention apart from 'cosmetic' features such as choosing the colour of the car or the type of cloth for the sofa.

Not so long ago the trend was the reverse of customization, using the same product for delivering different brands, so-called badge marketing. This technique was used by not-so-successful companies in the car industry such as British Leyland (now MG/ Rover) and General Motors and, more successfully, by white goods manufacturers such as Electrolux. This strategy, to put different names on essentially the same product in order to be able to charge different prices, is a short-sighted way to build sales and revenue that is unlikely to succeed in the longer term as it is based on 'fooling' the customers.

To avoid any misunderstandings – the practice of using the same parts to manufacture products for different brands is quite another matter. This sharing of parts is a production technique to reduce costs which makes a lot of sense as long as the profile of the brand is not diluted.

The reality is now that with flexible production methods it is possible to customize the product. You can buy a car in thousands of variants, some of which are cosmetic like colour, others more fundamental such as size, type of engine and interior seating plan. A Japanese bicycle company claims it can make and deliver 11,000 different variants.

Dell computers have done the same in the technology market. By changing the business model from 'first we make and then we sell' to 'first we sell and then we make', it can deliver a customized product made to your specification. It is of course worth noting that 'make' in this case equals 'assemble', but that is the case in many other industries as well. By customizing the product Dell's products are perceived as having a higher value than the competition.

In the service industry, customization is more common, although not always structured as such. Successful consultancy, one of the fastest growing sectors in business, thrives on providing a unique set of standard procedures for each client. The perception is one of total customization. The reality is that most successful consultancy companies operate with a fixed toolbox that is combined and modified to suit each client's requirements.

The third building block is to *communicate* in a way that is perceived as being 'just for me' without losing the economics of scale. At its most basic it is a question of individually addressed direct mail, at its sophisticated end it is to tailor the message and execution to the needs of each recipient. Amazon.com does the latter with its book recommendations. By tracking what the customer is buying, suggestions for further purchases are provided. The technique, conceptually, is no different from asking the local bookseller for recommendations, but as it is automatic and based on actual behaviour it is likely to deliver a suggestion of real interest.

Understand the target audience, develop and deliver a customized product and communicate in an individual-centred way.

CUSTOMIZED BRANDING IN BUSINESS-TO-BUSINESS MARKETING

For structural industry reasons, most business-to-business marketing is conducted in a different way to consumer goods marketing. The target audiences are often smaller, there are more personal contacts and personal selling, display advertising is less common, or at least the expenditures are lower, and traditionally the marketing departments have often played a role of marketing communication department rather than being responsible for integrated marketing.

Based on extensive experience of both sectors, it is possible to state categorically that in principle there are no major differences between marketing in business-to-business and business-to-consumer. However, there is one important *but* and that is that implementation in business-to-business marketing is often different to that in consumer marketing. The media are different, the demands are different, the marketing mix has a different emphasis, etc.

More companies have also come further down the road toward customized branding in business-to-business than in consumer marketing. The reason is, again, structural. It is easier to customize your offer, both in delivery and communication, if you deal with a smaller number of clients. If the business is selling nuclear power plants, the number of customers are limited, each product or service package is carefully customized to each individual customer, and in communicating with the client and the supplier has no doubt segmented the communication. Regulatory authorities get a message adapted to their circumstances – presumably focusing on safety – and the power company buying the unit gets a different message – perhaps focusing on financial benefits. Indeed, if heavy industry suppliers had been the drivers behind the marketing discipline, customized branding would be much more common.

From a competitive point of view it is consequently more important to fully understand customized branding in the business-to-business environment than in the consumer market. In the latter it is still possible 'to get away' with traditional marketing methods. While customized branding will in due course be the way all marketing is done, there is still some way to go. However, for business-to-business marketing, many more companies are applying elements of customized branding; so, unless the company is in a monopoly situation, the recommendation is to start to develop a customized branding strategy immediately.

Contrary to the opinion of many, a strong brand is much more important in a business-to-business environment than business to consumer. There are many reasons, but the main ones are that:

- The stakes, and risks, are higher. The risk of buying the wrong jar of coffee (cost of around £2.00) is considerably less than commissioning the wrong supplier to build a new factory for £100 million. If you buy the wrong coffee it is annoying, if you make a mistake with a major investment, your career may be in jeopardy, or even worse, the company's future may be affected. Even if the business-to-business decision is not in the £100 million category, the risks are there. Buying the wrong type of copying paper so that the printers of the company will need servicing more often, because the cheaper paper generates more dust, will not improve an executive's standing in the company. Even supplying the wrong vending machines for staff coffee can generate considerable antagonism.

- As a business buyer, or someone who is influencing or taking part in a buying decision, it is important to feel confident with the decision. A well-regarded brand provides that reassurance. The old saying 'No one ever got fired for buying an IBM computer' is perhaps no longer relevant but 'No one will be fired for choosing Microsoft' when it comes to PC software is. The well-established brands have an advantage far bigger than in the consumer market. Selling well-regarded branded goods to someone with 'a budget' has always been easier than selling to those who pay with their own money. In the latter case the propensity to take risks is higher than in the former.
- It is very important to be seen to make the right decision. In the company power game it is crucial to be seen to make the right decisions. It is important that the boss agrees with the decisions, but also peers, subordinates and those being involved in the purchase 'need' to feel that the decision made was 'the right thing to do'. The reasons are the same as in the previous point.

In this book, and in many other marketing books, consumer examples dominate. The reason is simply that we are all consumers and in many cases the use of well-known brands as examples are more relevant. This should not distract from the fact that brands and customized branding is very important to all business sectors. The principles are the same but the way to do it differs from sector to sector and category to category.

Brands and customized brands are more important in business-to-business than in consumer goods marketing.

To lead the market and stay market leader requires full commitment, persistence and discipline to follow the 'rules' of marketing described in this chapter. For sustainable progress this needs to be ingrained in the organization. It is not a quick fix but a philosophy that needs to be embraced by all.

4

Markets fragment, communication and competition increase, less time, more uncertainty

The purpose of this chapter is to outline some of the main factors in the marketplace driving business toward customized branding. There are of course many, many factors, this is but a selection of those considered the most important. By understanding the key elements behind a trend it is easier to define the right strategy and the right application correctly.

BRAND AND PRODUCT PROLIFERATION

In almost all market sectors we are witnessing an increase in the number of products and brands offered, markets are fragmenting and the choice is increasing. This is happening despite a consolidation in some market sectors among the suppliers. In the car industry Ford has bought Volvo and Jaguar, General Motors bought SAAB, Volkswagen bought Skoda, Seat and Bentley, to name a few. This consolidation at the corporate level is not replicated at the brand and product levels. All the above-mentioned brands still exist and within each main brand the number of subbrands and variants have increased. In the UK there are 52 brands of car for sale offering around 2,700 main model variants.

In a normal, European, large supermarket the number of products on the shelves have increased several times over during the last 25–30 years. In the UK, in the early 1970s you could find around 4,000 different items in a supermarket. This is now 25,000–30,000 items. This obviously has a great impact on the suppliers to the grocery trade and those companies competing in that industry, but it has also a great impact on society as a whole. Almost all of us visit a grocery store from time to time. We are in that role, as consumers, exposed to six to eight times as many items as only 25 years ago. This does of course not only influence how we behave in the grocery store but also in life in general. Each product category we are interested in and within each of those categories, we have less time than previously to consider the options available.

The numbers quoted above from the grocery trade is an indication of a general trend. Sector after sector see similar fragmentation. The number of banks and the products they offer as investment opportunities have multiplied in almost all countries; utilities like water and electricity, not to mention telephones, can be bought from a variety of sources while in the past there was one or two suppliers in each area. And, there is very little indicating that the trend will reverse. Over time, almost all markets fragment, at least as long as there is not a decline in total demand that can force some companies and brands out of a market.

The increase in choice, mainly through more variants within the same category, does not only influence the time available to consider each alternative. In many instances it also decreases customer loyalty. The more alternatives that are available, the greater the chance that you will choose something else. If only two products are available in a sector, the temptation to change is limited. If there are 20 alternatives, the temptation is much greater and the likelihood a customer will try a 'new' alternative increases. And when the 'tried and tested' brand has been abandoned once by a customer, the probability that this will happen again will increase. A loyal customer has turned into a promiscuous one who requires much more effort to keep loyal.

Markets fragment leading to more and more choice and competition.

THE EXPLOSION OF COMMUNICATION CHANNELS
AND MESSAGES

In the past you could watch one, two or maybe up to four television channels in each European country. Even the USA did not have more than three national networks 30 years ago although bigger cities also had a couple of local channels. Digital, satellite and cable technology has meant that today you can watch a new channel each day of the year if you have subscribed to enough television providers. Not many do that, but the increase in choice has put pressure on the established channels and opened up opportunities for new ones.

Television though, is not the only area. Radio has seen a similar explosion in many countries. While some traditional newspapers have disappeared, through lack of competitiveness, this has been more than compensated for by the launch of local neighbourhood newspapers and free newspapers. In total an increase. Similarly, traditional mainstream magazines have disappeared, but each old one has been replaced by several new special interest magazines. Fragmentation and specialization.

On top of this we have the new media such as the Internet and mobile telephones with an immense number of channels and messages.

More media leads to more messages, commercial and non-commercial. It was reported a couple of years ago that in the UK there are 32,000 products and services advertised in a year. It has also been reported that we are each, on average, hit by 3,000 commercial messages per day.

Such a deluge of information channels and messages subjects our brains to enormous pressure to handle the information. Fortunately for us, as humans, the brain ignores the majority of them. Unfortunately for us, as marketers, this means that the task of reaching the people we want to reach has become much more difficult resulting in more competition not only in the marketplace, as described above, but even more so in the mind space of the target audience where one brand's message is competing with all other brands plus news, gossip, scandals, sports, etc. An enormously competitive marketplace for messages.

Growth of communication channels, and more alternatives within each one, leads to intense competition for the customers' mind space.

NEW DISTRIBUTION CHANNELS

It is not only in these categories and media that there is proliferation. New channels to market have also appeared on the scene.

It used to be that if you wanted to buy a book, you went to the bookstore. Now you can also buy one via the Net or buy one in your local supermarket or even at the pharmacist's.

If you wanted to buy a car, you had to go to the local franchised dealer. If you went outside of the franchisee's district, the dealer had to refuse you a purchase. Now you can not only go to any franchised dealer you like, you can buy your car abroad if it is cheaper (in some European countries this can account for over 10% of new car sales), or you can go to the local supermarket, or buy one over the Net.

To make any financial transaction, even just to get some money or cash a cheque, you used to have to go to the bank, during its business hours of 9 a.m. to 3 p.m., in person, queue up and, after waiting, finally be served by a clerk. Nowadays, you can of course still go to the bank in person and opening hours are likely to have been extended, but it is more likely you will use any of the automated teller machines situated near the bank, or you can use the telephone, or your PC, or indeed the old-fashioned postal service.

It may seem like many of these changes took place a long time ago, but not so. In 1996 we recommended a leading UK high street bank (one of the 'big four' at the time) that they ought to focus on PC-banking, develop their service into what could be considered an Internet portal. The managers we talked to were not very enthusiastic, so we took the case to the business development director. The answer was 'no, people don't like to do this kind of thing with a computer, it is too slow. They like to use the telephone.' How wrong they were and how easy it would have been for the bank to have become a leader rather than a follower.

The diversity of distribution channels is a blessing for customized branding. It allows the company to customize how to deliver the product or service.

Fragmentation in distribution channels is a great opportunity for customized brands to reach the right customers in the right way.

THE SELECTIVE CUSTOMER

An important consequence of the increasing choice in supply, communication and delivery is that potential customers become even more selective, or choosy. If the car is only supplied in black, you just have to accept it. If all of a sudden other cars are available in all kinds of colours, and with extra features, the one supplying only black cars will lose out. As Henry Ford did when General Motors started to challenge Ford. If all of a sudden the IT department no longer has to use Microsoft products but can use Linux instead, the buyer is likely to be more choosy and more demanding.

In particular in the consumer markets, there has been an increase in the number of informed consumers, and the informed consumer is even more and better informed. People no longer take what the experts say for granted, not even when it comes to the family doctor. Rather than coming to the doctor and complaining about an illness, the informed consumer has searched the Internet for possible diagnosis and also searched the providers of medicine for the best cure prior to seeing the doctor.

The amateur expert has arrived in force, which unless the companies respond will lead to deterioration of trust in brands. What is required is of course information, and actively making it available to those who want to know, and keeping it away (but still accessible on demand) from those who are not interested.

Customers want to know but only when *they* are interested.

MORE UNCERTAINTY

All the trends mentioned above make brand management more difficult, or less effective. More choice and more media and distribution channels certainly make building a brand more complex.

On the other hand, a long-term trend, going in favour of active brand management, is the increasing perceived uncertainty of many people and the decreasing importance of family and friends. Higher workload, fewer community activities and more city life are just some of the factors leading to many individuals having a smaller close social circle than in the past. Perhaps many acquaintances but few real friends.

In the past many employees felt that they had a job for life with their employer. While it is not conclusively proven that employees change jobs more often now than they used to, there is a perception of job insecurity in most organizations. Equally, on the private side, the increase in divorces in parallel with more informal partnership arrangements (cohabiting, etc) have also contributed to a feeling of less certainty.

The need for someone to trust is, consequently, on the increase; so, it follows from this that a trustworthy brand is not only important but something some people may even actively seek out. Actually, when UK citizens were asked who or what they could trust, traditional consumer goods brands (Heinz, Kelloggs, Nestlé) and retailers (Boots, Marks & Spencer) came high up the list. In a world which is constantly seen to be changing, the 'good old trusted' brands are still there.

To be in a position of trust is of course a great advantage in a competitive world. If it is possible to increase that element of trust by doing the right things, providing interesting products or seen to be caring and perhaps even entertaining, much is to be gained.

The more uncertainty, the more welcome is a trusted brand.

Many of the factors mentioned above are more likely to make life difficult for the marketing executive than making it easy. However, there are also plenty of opportunities. The main task, though, is to recognize what the trends are. By understanding what is going on, the problems can be turned into opportunities, especially for those who are leading the way.

5

We are all different, but not that different – the principles of segmentation

Customized branding is a process to adapt the brand to each individual's special circumstances, whether as a professional buyer or decision maker, or a consumer. Segmentation has two important roles in this process. The first one is to help brand management understand the customer base by clustering similar individuals to define current customers better and to get guidance on where to find new ones. The second role is as a tool for implementing the customized brand proposition, in other words to define, develop, communicate and deliver the customized brand proposition to groups of people rather than individuals.

The principles of segmentation are straightforward like most things in marketing, but equally, again like most things, they are difficult to do well. The following is just a short introduction as the subject will be covered from different angles throughout the book – segmentation is a core subject in the curriculum for customized branding.

THE BASIC RATIONALE

The *average person does not exist*, or at least there are very few of them. If the average number of visits to a supermarket per household per month is 5, but the 5 is made up of one-half coming 3 times and the other half coming 7 times, building a strategy around the 'fact' that the average is 5 will be highly misleading. Using averages will lead to an average brand – not good enough for being or staying number one.

Each individual likes to be treated as such, and increasingly so as described earlier. Individual marketing is, however, in most cases impractical and expensive. If there are thousands of customers and each has to be treated with total individual care and attention, it will require a large number of people to do it. This in itself will make it expensive, but what will make it even more expensive is to provide an individually made special version for each customer and then personally communicate and deliver the goods or services. There are, of course, sectors where this is a viable option. Financial services for high-value individuals, fashion for the rich, selling very expensive holidays or motor cars are a few examples. But these examples are not relevant to large and more mainstream markets. Most brands cannot afford personal individual attention to thousands or even millions of customers.

How can this dilemma of individual attention and costs be solved? Fortunately, perfect individual attention is not necessary because we are not that different. We are different but not uniquely so. By categorizing the target audience into segments based on selected criteria, it all becomes much more easy to understand and manage, and much more financially viable. This is the only reason for using segmentation.

The main challenge of segmentation is to find criteria that are relevant to the market sector in question. This can be life stages (for markets such as home furnishing), income level (financial services products), gender and age (sanitary protection and sports products), type of dwelling (home insurance), lifestyle (holidays and fashion), etc. It can also be based on the consumption of certain products, like motor oil and car ownership or travel insurance and holidays. As will be illustrated in this chapter, just one segmentation criteria is rarely enough.

We can all slip into suitable segments.

THE RAW MATERIAL

To be able to segment a market, it is necessary to possess the raw material. The raw material is usually data that describe the relationship between the segmentation criteria and individuals or, for business-to-business marketing, individuals and the company they are working for.

The material can come from many different sources, internal databases collecting customer behaviour and sales and/or external information such as life stage information or customer classification systems such as Acorn or Mosaic. Without good raw material it is very difficult to segment.

The best is to have comprehensive customer data. In consumer markets this can be generated via so-called loyalty cards often used in retailing and in the travel sector, or if the company is in direct contact with the customer can be generated via invoicing systems (especially, of course, in business-to-business marketing), but telephone, banking and utility companies (such as electricity, water and gas suppliers), among others, have such data sources as well.

The quality of the data is of course important, but it is also important that it covers a reasonable amount of the company's transactions. It is often impossible to cover all transactions – and it is not necessary to do so – but at least 50% of transactions, and ideally 80%, are required. To collect 100% is hardly worthwhile if it entails additional costs.

Customer data are the raw material for effective segmentation.

MULTILEVEL SEGMENTATION

Most segmentation is 1-dimensional – as in the examples mentioned in the previous section. On the basis of one dimension, everyone in the target audience is classified, and then this information is used for marketing activities. This is the traditional method. In some cases that may well be sufficient, but to build a customized brand it is probably not enough.

Value/month	500+	250–500		–250
Frequency/month	3+	1–3		–1
Recency	Last month	Others		
Life stage	Single/ couple	Family with children	Empty-nesters	Pensioners
Lifestyle	Four to six categories			

Figure 5.1

A much more in-depth understanding of the target group will be achieved by applying a multilevel segmentation model. Such segmentation is based on applying different criteria and doing the selection in several stages.

Figure 5.1 shows a typical grocery retailer as an example. This segmentation model has three main levels and within the first level there are three different dimensions. The first level is based on shopping behaviour. The first of the three dimensions is value: how much has each customer bought per month. This information is important in order to identify what belongs to the best, second-best and, in this case, third-best value groups.

The ability of a model to predict and help in influencing future behaviour is an essential part of the concept. To segment on the basis of what people have done is 'easy', it is just a question of collecting information and processing it. It is considerably more difficult to segment in such a way that it becomes possible to predict future behaviour, making the segmentation process a tool for improving future business, to know what to say and deliver, to whom and how.

The second dimension, frequency, is one way of isolating an indicator of future behaviour and business potential. In the case of a retailer, the more often a customer comes to the shop, the more likely it is that the customer will buy something. Frequency is not all that interesting from a historical point of view, but to find customers who may buy more is an important piece of information.

The third dimension is recency – when did the customer last

visit the shop. If someone used to buy a lot and came frequently but has not visited the shop for the last three months, it is unlikely that this customer is a very good prospect. On the other hand, if the last visit was recently, chances are that the customer will come again soon, or at least can be encouraged to do so.

By adding frequency and recency to value, a fuller picture of the customer is emerging. The predictability has increased. But the picture does not have a lot of depth. This information may well be enough to generate an efficient sales promotion campaign, but to use it as a strategic tool for building a customized brand, more is required. It is only the first step, a way to identify which customers are likely to be the best customers in the future.

Life stage information is the second level in this example. In this case there are four life stages, it could be many more (10–15 different ones are not unusual). Life stage is another traditional determinator of behaviour. Your age and family structure says a lot about you. The needs of a young single person are very different from those of a young family, although of the same age. The empty-nester has a different perspective from a pensioner.

Personal data, such as male or female, are also to be considered in this context, of course. Research by the UK Royal Mail has confirmed that males and females do react differently to different creative executions but with one notable exception. In financial services, traditionally a 'male' sphere of interest, females over 30 were so conditioned to read 'male' advertising and direct mail that they have accepted this style as generic and consequently there was no noticeable, immediate advantage in applying a 'female' profile to the creative execution.

By combining the first and second levels the usefulness of the customer data increases dramatically, especially for planning tactical activities such as a direct mail campaign with a set of special offers. A low-value customer can all of a sudden be an interesting customer if the retailer can deduce that the amount spent is actually that household's total grocery spend. This is a 100% loyal customer. Such a customer is much more valuable than one spending the same amount, but is a member of a big family and consequently only spends a fraction of total spend at the store. The big family may only buy the 'bargain' items (with lower margin) while the 100% loyal customer buys all, generating a better margin for the retailer. The totally loyal customer is also more valuable because he or she will cost less to retain as a customer for the future and is more likely to stay true to the brand.

The strategy is different as well for the two types of customer. For the 100% customer it is plainly to keep the customer happy. There is no need to try to get the person to spend more because there is no more share of wallet to be gained. On the other hand, in the big family case there is a lot to be gained by increasing share of wallet. But will this succeed if the customer spends only a limited amount? And, will the necessary investment in promotional costs be worthwhile?

Life stage information on its own can be very useful in order, for instance, to customize marketing communication, and value/frequency/recency paints a good picture of the potential of different customer groups. The two levels together further improve the usefulness, not only tactically as described above, but also strategically. The information can be used for tracking business development. Is the customer profile as expected? What is the profile of the heavy users?, etc.

The third level of this model is lifestyle. It could also have been socio-economic information or perhaps even a geographical segmentation. It all depends on what is possible and what is required. A 'soft' dimension such as lifestyle or attitudes can add considerable depth to a segmentation model. It may not be needed for all activities, but to understand the lifestyle of a person and from that deduce what these people actually would like to have, can be most rewarding for a company.

The three levels provide different segmentation dimensions. Each individual customer can be classified in three different ways, and within the first level in three different dimensions. For a segmentation model to be solid enough to be used for customizing the brand, one level is rarely enough, so the additional dimensions need to be built into the model as illustrated above.

Multi-level segmentation brings life and usefulness to the customer data.

SEGMENTATION PRINCIPLES

Segmentation is not a new concept, but in the context of custom-ized branding there are a few principles worthy of special mention.

The first principle is that *segmentation is a tool for inclusion, not exclusion*. To focus on just one segment can in the short term be very profitable, but it assumes that (a) the business has limited ambitions and (b) that the world will forever stay the same. Banks traditionally spend relatively large amounts on recruiting young customers on the principle that once a customer with a bank, it is unlikely the individual will change later in life (as it is seen to be so complicated to change). Such a strategy is to segment for inclusion and is likely to pay dividends in the longer term.

Other financial institutions, or even the same ones that spend money recruiting students, actively discourage certain categories to be or stay customers because they 'cost too much'. Similar strategies, which exclude low-profit customers and pamper high-profit ones, have been suggested by a number of manage-ment consultancies and CRM (customer relationship manage-ment) promoters. The strategy may well pay dividends short term. Long term it is a recipe for disaster.

For a brand or company with ambitions to be a leader such a short-term strategy is incompatible with brand leader ambitions, unless the strategy is to be a 'snob' brand. American Express in Europe applied for many years a philosophy of rejecting many applicants to build the snob value – apparently with great success at the time. To grow outside of the premium market and become a generally acknowledged leader is, however, not possible on this basis. First, it creates ill will – who wants to be rejected? The Halifax, one of the biggest banks in the UK, gained a considerable amount of ill will when its selection strategy became common knowledge, and it had to make a public apology – and reverse the strategy. Second, it is short-sighted. Who knows which customers will be profitable in the future? IKEA, the world's leading home furnishing store, has a strategic cornerstone that it is for 'everyone'. No one is to be excluded, especially not because they are poor or because they are not currently in the home furnishing market. Because every customer counts even if the purchases are low, one day, who knows, they might become a 'big' customer.

The sensible, long-term approach is to adapt the brand proposition to the different categories. It is to use the methods of customized branding to make the proposition interesting and relevant for both supplier and customer. One day the customer may move to another segment of the market, and the loyalty gained from providing an interesting offer when money was tight will be rewarded with many purchases.

Segmentation is *an internal technique* for brand management, not for external use. A customer is only interested in personal attention. A customer is not interested in the classifications used for allocating different types of customer. The only exception may be to be told that 'you are among our best customers'. For a customer to know that he or she is a 'middle' or 'low' value customer is unlikely to build any brand value, rather the reverse. There are a few exceptions to this principle. The airline industry is one such exception, where customers appear to accept classifications although only when it comes to total value. If lifestyle were also colour-coded and shown on the card, many would most probably be upset.

The segmentation process is only a way to process information so that a suitable brand proposition can be developed, communicated and delivered. It is crucial to the credibility of the company that this understanding is maintained all the time, and one way of doing this is to have an attitude of individual attention, an implementation built around the individual and common sense among all staff, especially those in direct contact with the customers.

Segmentation models such as the one shown above can potentially be seen as manipulation. To avoid this it is of course essential to *follow all relevant guidelines and if appropriate introduce more stringent ones* to protect consumer and customer privacy, and only use the data for the purpose of delivering a better product. Tesco, the leader in this field, states clearly that the reward it gives users of the Tesco Clubcard is a thank you for sharing information. It is also obvious to the Tesco customers that it is a better store. It may not be obvious to everyone that this is the result of their customer information, but, if asked, Tesco managers can give a straight answer. By the same token any customer will object to being manipulated. If a customer normally buys Nescafé Gold Blend and a couple of weeks after purchasing Gold Blend gets a special money-off coupon through the post for the main competitor Kenco or the retailer's own label product, this is not a clever way of using data. However, to give the Gold Blend user a money-off coupon on a bigger jar of Gold Blend is to understand the customer.

Finally, segmentation for customizing a brand is *not an exact science*. It is 'grey', not black and white. It is sometimes based on what are only assumptions, not necessarily exact facts. On the other hand, marketing activities are not predictable to the last decimal point, far from it, because they involve people. From this it follows that it is often better to use an imperfect model that is relatively easy to develop and follow than a more perfect one that will take months or even years to develop.

This fact can often cause problems in the relationships between brand marketing and IT departments who are processing the data required for the segmentation. The answer is simple. To succeed with a customized brand strategy these problems have to be overcome. Flair and creativity should thrive on segmentation and data, not be drowned or delayed because of it.

Remember, segmentation:

- **is a tool for inclusion, not exclusion;**
- **is an internal technique, keep it away from customers;**
- **methods have to follow all relevant guidelines for the company to retain credibility;**
- **is not an exact science. It is different shades of grey, not digitally black and white.**

THE ECONOMICS OF SEGMENTATION

The purpose of segmentation is to get closer to the customer, yet to retain the economies of scale by dealing with large numbers of people at any one time. By dealing with defined segments, rather than individuals, the company gets economies of scale effects not otherwise possible.

As to segmentation in itself, the principle is simply that the cost of segmentation must be covered by increases in profits that at least cover those costs. The sensible manager makes sure that the gain is considerably more than the segmentation cost to have a safety margin in case the sales increase will be less than forecasted.

A key element of ensuring that costs are kept under control and the economies of scale are utilized is to make sure that the size of each segment is large enough to make customization worthwhile. The size of each segment has to be in relation to the business potential. For a high-turnover/profit potential group the segments can be smaller than for a low-turnover/profit potential group.

For newcomers to segmentation based on customer data, it is easy to get carried away by all the possibilities. However, to split a customer group into 43 different segments is a waste of time as it is impossible and unproductive to work with such a wide range. Between 3 and 6 segments is a good starting point, and staying at that level allows all involved to keep track of the segments. In due course, subsegments within the main groups can be developed if appropriate, but the experience is that this rarely happens in practice. Even Tesco with its sophisticated approach apparently rarely applies more than 12 segments, although it has been claimed Tesco can define 1 million different segments among its 8 million active customers.

Segmentation has to pay for itself and ensure economies of scale.

Segmentation is only of relevance as a means to an end, and that is to better understand the customer, or potential customer universe, and to make implementation of a customized branding strategy workable in practice. How sophisticated the segmentation model needs to be depends of course on the market situation and the brand profile, but it makes sense to take one step at a time, building knowledge of the customers and the implementation processes.

6
Find the Big Number

Most companies have too much data available to them. These data may not all be used, but if all data and information are put together, they represent in most cases an enormous amount of numbers and other facts. If a company has 100,000 customers and each customer buys 10 items 10 times per year, that in itself will generate $100,000 \times 10 \times 10 = 10,000,000$ records. And most companies have much more than that.

Analysis paralysis is often the result of data overflow. It has been alleged that one UK retailer has an analysis team of 40 top analysts working with the customer data generated by a customer card; they do not achieve any useful insights as the perfect, all-encompassing data model is very difficult to handle.

The answer to this problem is to look for the main opportunity, and the way to do this is to search for the 'Big Number' – a concept we have introduced to make strategy based on customer data effective. This chapter is an introduction to the subject.

WHAT IS THE BIG NUMBER?

Business and marketing strategy is not a mathematical science. It is, as explained earlier, 'grey'. That is why the concept of a Big Number is so useful as it simplifies the 'numbers game', it pulls out what is really important and allows everyone to forget about the rest. The danger is that, with vast amounts of data, there is always something new and interesting emerging. Chasing all these trails will lead nowhere and the focus will be lost.

The power of the Big Number lies in its single-mindedness. This makes it easy to focus on the issue at stake, easy for all to understand and a powerful tool to rally a team around a specific task.

For a Big Number to be useful it must answer a Big Question – a key strategic issue for the brand. It could be simple things like penetration and repeat purchase frequency, or more complex ones like share of trade among poor people or, for a food retailer, the number of claimed vegetarians actually eating meat products.

> For one company we worked with, the question was one of expansion. By reviewing available data, the conclusion was that there was a particular channel to market that had been ignored by most competitors. With the help of this channel, the company could reach up to 2 million new prospective customers. Two million became the Big Number leading to an innovative distribution strategy.

The Big Number delivers focus.

FROM BIG NUMBER TO BIG IDEA

The Big Number is an excellent handle for a creative brief. It crystallizes the key issue and makes it easy to work with. A crucial part of the creative process is to find the right focus. The Big Number delivers that.

> For one European food retailer, the Big Number was the number of 'hard-up' people shopping in the stores. At a head office, in nice offices filled with well-paid people getting excited about excellent premium food products to be launched, it is easy to forget that there are hard-up people – and they want to buy cheap products. Not

because they like to, but because they have to. By studying purchase data, it was apparent that 15% of all customers fell into the 'super value' segment. The Big Idea coming out of the Big Number was to develop a range more appropriate in price level, choice and quality for this category of customer.

This may not, in retrospect, seem like an earth-shattering idea, and in the sense of originality it wasn't. But, first, it had not been done before. Second, the focus on a Big Number made the idea bigger in the minds of the project team as well as the rest of the company – which helped the development and implementation process. Third, because of the scope of the idea, some unique and aggressive solutions were introduced as part of the concept. Fourth, it was a success.

With a Big Number, the Big Idea is not far away.

FROM BIG NUMBER AND BIG IDEA TO BIG BRAND

Not all big numbers lead to a Big Idea and not all big ideas lead to a Big Brand. In some cases it may 'just' lead to the brand surviving. However, big ideas do help to build big brands with or without the big number as a tool to focus the minds of all involved.

For one food product supplier we worked with, the Big Number was the share of its business that was carried out under a label that was essentially a generic one: a house brand plus a product description. This was a considerable competitive weakness, as the market sector was full of strongly branded competitors, and at the time one new, very strong competitor was expected to enter the market. The company thought it was a brand marketing company but it turned out that 70% of turnover was in products without a well-defined brand. Identifying this as a single number led to a crash programme to develop proper brands leading to an increase in business by 20% in one of the sectors, and that the new competitive threat never got a foot-hold.

Big Ideas build Big Brands.

HOW DO YOU FIND A BIG NUMBER?

The process to find the Big Number is one of creative analysis. To move from a giant data warehouse full of numbers to just one numerical symbol is a distinct skill. Just looking at the numbers will not deliver a Big Number.

The first step is to understand the context, what is the Big Question facing the brand. The second step is to distil all the data in a process by applying a combination of experience, creativity and an ability to know what to look for. Both to find a Big Number and to assess whether it is the right number do require a fair amount of experience. It is not a game for newly qualified MBAs but for experienced executives who know what to look for and can assess what information is likely to be useful on the track to finding the Big Number.

The Big Number can be found in a customer data summary table, in a market research report or a sales summary. It may even be in the profit and loss accounts. It is usually the result of a combination of two or three numbers, dividing for instance sales of one product by the number of customers in a certain segment and comparing this with a heavy user group.

It takes experience to find a Big Number.

The concept of the Big Number is based on a combination of the quest for simplicity and making data useful and understandable for all those outside the analysis and IT departments. It is, though, reasonable to issue a warning. It is essential to base the Big Number on sound analysis and reasoning because if the Big Number is the wrong number, the company will waste a lot of resources and time. However, get it right, and the Big Number can be a tool to move mountains – quickly.

7
The 10 steps to a customized brand

The purpose of this chapter is to give an overview of the different steps as a guide to building a customized brand marketing plan.

THE STEPS

The 10 steps can be divided into three overall stages.

Stage 1 Understanding	The category and the competition The customers The company and the brand
Stage 2 Developing the brand proposition	Adapting the brand proposition to each segment
Stage 3 Implementation	Product development Distribution Pricing Communication Promotion Selling

The first stage is about understanding. Understanding the category and the competition (Step 1), the customers (Step 2) and the company and the brand (Step 3). To be able to create customized brand propositions, it is crucial to have a solid understanding of the business dynamics. For traditional brand marketing it sometimes is enough just to have flair and creativity, but to do a proper customization job, detailed knowledge is required.

The second stage is at the core of the process (Step 4). To define the brand proposition by segments forms the basis for all marketing activities that will follow. Step 4 is about how to adapt the singular brand platform into x number of segments. It also covers how to keep the brand together as a cohesive unit, as it is easy to go off the rails in all kinds of different directions with a customized brand. For the brand to remain a brand this must be avoided.

The third stage is about implementation. What is the point of having excellent understanding and a great brand platform if the implementation does not work? The implementation skills often make or break a brand.

While it is impossible to cover all the aspects of brand management implementation in one book, the different chapters provide an insight into what is of particular importance, what to do and sometimes what not to do within each type of activity. The subject matter goes from developing the product or service (Step 5), through distribution (Step 6), pricing (Step 7), communication (Step 8), promotion (Step 9) and selling (Step 10). Last but not least, what will the results be, and why?

THE CUSTOMIZED BRAND PLAN

Most companies spend far too much time on developing plans, and not enough on understanding customers and implementation. However, it is of course necessary to document the brand strategy in some sort of plan. The starting point is a normal brand plan, and the customization is then integrated into the framework with particular emphasis on defining the key segments and, of course, describing the brand proposition by segment.

Most brand plans are written as a static document, which is based on a snapshot at the time of the plan, and the implementation is based on the circumstances at that particular time. This has never been a particularly efficient way to operate as the circumstances do not stay the same over time. It is already a problem for traditional brand marketing, but for a customized brand the problems multiply due to its more complex structure and can easily lead to lost opportunities.

The plan for a customized brand must contain a dynamic element. We do not live in a static world. The competitive scene changes, customers change, technology changes, etc. If the brand management has built the plan on customer data, it has a superb tool for dynamic planning. To not use that is to lose an excellent opportunity for more effective marketing.

To manage the dynamic process requires, first, an active system for follow-up, monitoring what is going on. How are the different segments doing? Are the key indicators developing in the right direction? Any warning signs?

Second, mechanisms to act on the signals from the follow-up systems need to be in place. Whether this involves management meetings or ongoing reviews by individual executives is irrelevant as long as it works and something is actually done. This includes ways to reallocate resources from one segment to another, or from one type of activity to another, say from product development to communication.

Third, the management information system, whether formal or informal, must recognize this flexibility, and positively encourage it. Otherwise, the dynamics required will not materialize.

This may sound like a recipe for total anarchy. It is not. The flexibility and creativity must take place against a structured background. The thinking must be systematic, the end result clearly defined. It is improvization of a set tune. How to get there is up to the 'musician', the more extensive the improvization the better, but if the underlying tune is lost and it is not possible to recognize the basis for improvization, then it does not work.

Developing and managing a customized brand is a dynamic process.

THE DR JEKYLL AND MR HYDE REQUIREMENT

Successful brand management requires a mix of being systematic and precise (Dr Jekyll) and creative and approximate (Mr Hyde). If everything is just systematic and precise, there will be no innovations, no creative sparkle. If it is just full of creativity and approximations, profitability will suffer and the company as a whole will despair over brand management's flow of erratic ideas.

Customizing the brand puts this requirement to even tougher tests. Handling data and analysing customer behaviour requires a systematic approach. Splitting marketing budgets across more segments and dealing with sometimes fairly small clusters of customers does require attention to detail as mistakes can multiply.

On the other hand, customized branding not only requires that one brand platform is developed, but that this brand platform also needs to be adapted to each segment. Products and services need adaptation. To cope with all this requires both creativity and the skill to make approximations at the right time. To be able to react quickly, it is impossible to do a 100% thorough analysis. And, it is not necessary as the marketing activities are not 100% predictable anyway. The ability to approximate at the right level, and to look at things in detail when required (for instance, when evaluating a new product's P&L), is also an important skill in this context.

One major reason for the failure of many companies to utilize customer data fully to build a customized brand is the conflict between the IT world's digital I/O or 100% precision way of working and marketing's approximation approach (as described earlier). More than one major UK retailer has failed or has had the full implementation delayed several years because of not being able to bridge this gap.

The world of customized branding is not black and white. It is sometimes grey, more often multi-coloured. It is an application of 'fuzzy' thinking. 'Good enough' and quick is often better than 'absolutely correct' and 'we will be ready in 6 months' time'. However, as with the Big Number, to be able to make approximations the right way, experience is crucial. It is not for the newly hired junior brand manager to make approximations, it is for the experienced senior manager.

The brand customization process is not digitally black and white but approximate and multi-coloured based on a structured process.

NEW AND OLD BRANDS

Most applications of customized branding methods concern established brands or extensions of established brands. Tesco used customer data to launch Tesco personal finance, a new venture as such, but from a brand marketing point of view a range extension; presumably customer data to support the launch plan came from Tesco's retail customers. The reason is that, first, customizing the brand is easiest if customer data is available, and customer data is of course not available, unless the brand is already on the market.

The second aspect is that to customize a brand there must be a brand platform to customize. However, this is not necessary. It is perfectly possible to start with a customized plan from the beginning but it is highly unusual. One reason is that the brand manager may not have the basic brand platform right. The expected customers may not materialize but others will. The first mainstream customers of mobile phones were not the rich bankers but builders, plumbers and other craftsmen who needed to be reachable at all times and were never close to a traditional phone.

Third, most brands are old brands; there are very few successful new brands. Coca-Cola and Levi's are over 100 years old and even Microsoft and Nike are over 25 years old. It is also more profitable to develop and enhance an existing brand than launch a new one. Customized branding allows management to revitalize existing brands, breathe new life into brands that have a wide following and as a consequence generate considerable additional profits for the brand owners.

A customized brand can be new or old but it is a great way to improve profitability of an existing brand.

DESIRE? PROFITS?

To build a highly desirable brand with customization methods takes an approach that is a mix of multi-coloured approximations and systematic thinking. Sustainable profits require follow-up and enough time, but never more, to get it 'about' right. Customizing a brand is an excellent way of improving the profitability and longevity of established brands.

8

Step 1: know the enemy and the battlefield

Marketing is a fight for market share, market growth, increasing turnover and profits, and sometimes survival. To fight without knowing the enemy, the competition, is not very clever. That is why the road to understanding starts with the enemy, the competition.

Not knowing where the enemy is makes fighting very difficult. That is why defining the battlefield, the category, is a fundamental, first building block of the process to understand competition.

The two dimensions, competition and category, are interlinked, but for simplicity's sake they are treated separately below – although in the same chapter – and the purpose of this chapter is to provide some basic advice on the subject. Only a few key elements are covered as the subject matter is, or should be, part of any marketing textbook.

COMPETITION

Who you are competing with defines to a large extent who you are, and where you are coming from. Trying to beat a defined set of brands influences the fighter's way of fighting, understanding of the universe and what to learn.

A competitive analysis does not require more special skills than a will to see the world from another angle than one's own:

- Who are the competitors? Names? Size? Ownership?
- Who are their customers? Key segments? Loyal or promiscuous customers?
- What do they do? What products and services do they provide? How much are they selling? Where do they make money?
- Why do they do what they do? The historical context? Where do they come from? What is the culture?
- Why are they successful?
- And so on.

There are many questions – most are easy to answer. The most difficult question to answer honestly is usually 'why is brand *x* successful?'. To give an objective assessment of a competitive brand is for many a 'mental block' but one that needs to be overcome. There is always a good reason, and the clearer that understanding is, the more likely it is that it will be possible to defeat that brand in due course.

Understanding who the competition's customers are is always of use but even more so if the strategy is to customize the brand. Segmenting the competitor's customer base and then defining the key aspect of each segment can provide very useful information and insights for developing a brand proposition by segment that just might wipe out competitive positions.

Most companies fail in one important aspect of competitive analysis, and that is in documenting the findings and then continuously following up on what the competition is doing. An analysis once a year is standard in most companies, but more often than not the analysis starts from scratch each year. It is much more efficient to monitor what is going on consistently and then conclude whenever there is a significant development or specific reason. A competitor may close down; another one may enter the market. One competitor may launch a successful new service, others may stagnate.

Competitors usually think in similar ways, so it is safe to assume that (a) the competition is always planning something new, (b) the competition is not stupid, ignorant or incapable (yes, I have heard all these in some very reputable companies) but is approximately as good a company as any, and (c) if a new innovation is on its way to the market, other companies have probably also considered similar ideas.

It is only by knowing the enemy you will have a chance of beating the enemy.

THE CATEGORY

Defining the category is a classical marketing challenge. The marketing textbooks are full of examples of successful and not so successful examples. The train companies in the USA who thought they were in the train business and not the transport business. Volvo once thought their future was not in the safe car business but in the leisure business. Mercedes thought they were in the engineering business and not in the mid-range luxury car business. Disney realized they were not in the animated film business but the entertainment and dream business.

Getting the category right is crucial to the whole brand marketing process, customized or not. Just like all other aspects of branding, the real answers are in the minds of the customers. Volvo really did think at one stage that they were on their way to becoming a leisure business, and as a consequence invested in a range of leisure companies. Of course, it did not work as Volvo is a car and truck company. Mercedes-Benz bought a number of engineering companies with very limited success. A marmalade company thought they were in the 'spreads' business, and as a consequence launched peanut butter. Of course, it did not work as consumers don't buy spreads, they buy marmalade or peanut butter, not marmalade and peanut butter. And, consumers do not go around thinking 'I am going to buy some spreads' – they think 'I want to buy some marmalade.'

Disney's transformation from an animation studio to an entertainment giant was a result of insight and understanding what films (and in particular the classical Disney films) are really about – being entertained. Skilled and very consistent implementation has of course helped to create the success.

> Disney theme park employees are not working in the park, they are 'on stage' – whether dressed up as Mickey Mouse and Donald Duck or cleaning the streets or serving soft drinks, it is a show!

As the category is formed in the minds of the customers, it may change from person to person. For the overall brand platform, the category has to be defined with a majority, or macro, perspective. Coca-Cola is a drink, aiming to take a share of throat and increase its business at the expense of coffee, tea and not least tap water. That is the macro-perspective. For some the perspective is much narrower. Coca-Cola is in the US drinks category, the Cola drink category or it may even be, for some, only in the fast-food soft drink category.

These subsectors need to be explored for the benefit of adapting the brand proposition. For Coca-Cola the fast-food soft drink category may be an important subsector, with specific brand requirements, certainly distribution requirements and also pricing policy requirements.

By understanding the category, and with it the competition, it will be possible to map the market dynamics. What makes the market develop and change? What are the key drivers? Which customers matter most, who are the trendsetters when driving the market forward? Some market segments may have a disproportionate influence, a traditional example being journalists when it comes to fashion.

With all this comes the necessity to understand the quantitative parts of the category: What is the size of the market? What is the growth rate, if any? What is growing and what is in decline? What are the product and customer splits? What is the price and margin structure? Who makes money where? All these questions go with defining a market and are part of basic marketing practice.

If you don't know the battlefield, the category, you will not know where to fight.

DESIRE? PROFITS?

Desirability is a concept of relativity. One brand is seen in relation to others, not in isolation. To be the chosen, desired brand, the brand must be seen to be more attractive than the other brands. To get to this position is not possible unless the 'others' are well defined. To avoid waste, focus is necessary. Focusing on the 'important' competitors and the 'right' category is fundamental not only to a prosperous business but also for efficient use of marketing funds.

9
Step 2: know your customers

It is, of course, important to know the customers of a brand when developing marketing strategies and activities, and much has been written about how to do it. The purpose of this chapter is, however, to give some key guidelines and perspectives on how to do this as part of developing a customized brand.

WHY?

The simple answer to this question is: 'How can one do without it?' However, that is not a particularly enlightening answer.

Every business needs to know its customers to be able to serve them in the right way. It is not possible to conclude what people want without proper knowledge. The standard and amount of customer knowledge differs considerably from industry to industry. A bank or a retailer has the potential to know more than a supplier of cucumbers or copperwire to the consumer market does.

Even within the same industry there are considerable differences in the level of customer knowledge. In retailing Tesco knows a lot more than the discount chain Netto, British Airways know more than the low-price airline Ryanair. This has nothing necessarily to do with ability but with business strategy. If the brand platform is based on a low price alone, most companies with that kind of strategy just wait for the bargain hunters to come, as the business model does not allow for customer analysis. On the other hand if the strategy is to have a brand with more depth, more knowledge is required to achieve that.

To know the customers is not only to know the existing customers but all potential customers. The better the understanding is of the existing customers, the easier it is to get to understand where future customers are to be found. 'It is easier to find what you are looking for if you know what you are looking for.' By carefully looking at the existing customer base, we can sometimes find pointers to new customer categories.

A classical, and old, example is the launch of the Ford Mustang. The Ford Mustang, as revolutionary in its time as the Chrysler Viper in the 1990s, was initially aimed at the young and fairly wealthy. Ford soon discovered after the launch that although some young people did buy the car this target group was rather small and the big potential was to be found among middle-aged men who had always wanted a sports car but had not been able to afford one earlier. The strategy was soon adapted to the new realities and the car went on to become a great success.

For a customized brand strategy a thorough and comprehensive customer understanding is a prerequisite. It is by understanding the customer universe, including the universe of potential customers, that it will be possible to devise a customized strategy. After all, if you don't know the customers, how can you customize?

If you do not know your customers and can't do anything about it, stop reading now!

WHERE TO FOCUS?

All customers are of course not equal, nor are we all average. While the purpose of segmentation is to be able to include, not exclude, it is important to put the emphasis in the right place. Focus is necessary.

For any business it is the best customers that matter. They are more profitable as they buy more but usually do not cost much more to keep as a customer. While we should not exclude anybody, to focus on the key customer groups when developing the business is crucial. It is the 'heavy users' who matter. Something beer companies discovered a long time ago: heavy users of beer behave differently than the average and if the brand strategy is based around the average, the heavy users will feel alienated, while the reverse does not hold true.

It is however crucial to understand the difference between focusing on best customers and excluding the not so good customers. The latter is bad business practice as outlined earlier. The former is good business practice because it puts the focus on the people who matter: 'Anybody is welcome but we run our business so that we are sure that our best customers will like it.'

What is a 'best customer' and what is the proportion of best customers of all customers? This differs from industry to industry. For one fashion retailer the top 15% accounted for 80+% of turnover. For a grocery retailer 50% accounted for 80% of turnover. Pareto's principle of 20% accounting for 80% is often a good starting point.

To establish the Pareto curve we need to know what share of business the biggest customer accounts for, then the second biggest and so on. This is the first analysis to do to understand the customer base. With the help of the curve it is possible to isolate the best customers so that the brand can be developed to the needs of these best customers, rather than the 'average'.

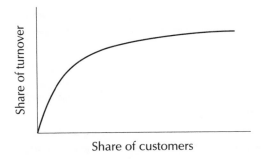

At a quick glance it may seem more appropriate to classify customers according to total profit than total turnover. Perhaps surprisingly, it is usually wrong to base the classification on profit. The reason lies in a misunderstanding of the suppliers' role and that of the customers'.

From an aggressive brand strategy point of view the most important element of customer behaviour is to establish contact with the supplier through visiting, calling, responding to email or whatever means is used. Without a contact, nothing can happen. The second most important element is that the customer buys. This comes second because without a contact there is no possibility of purchase. A contact, or acceptance of contact, and a purchase by the customer is what is expected in response to being presented with a proposition. Consequently the level of contact or size of purchase are key selection criteria.

It is the role of the supplier to offer the potential customer something that is sufficiently interesting and desirable (a) to establish a contact and (b) to lead to a purchase. Whether this purchase is profitable or not is not a selection criteria as it is the task of the supplier's management to optimize the profitability.

Using profitability as a selection criterion leads to passive management because the management of profitability across the range has effectively been abdicated to the customers. On the other hand, focusing on the number of contacts and purchases leads to proactive and aggressive marketing and management because the propositions that appeal to people have to be delivered in a cost-effective way for the company to prosper.

This is why for instance successful retailers do not use profitability as a selection criteria but focus on visitor frequency and turnover.

The first step toward a customized brand strategy is to differentiate between those who really matter, the best customers, and those who will have to accept what has been concluded on behalf of the best customers. The main brand platform has to be developed with the best customers in mind. For the others, the brand can be customized but only when the primary group has been taken care of.

Focus on your best customers, let the rest follow.

HOW TO DO IT

To make understanding the customers a manageable process two things are required. Information/data and a tool to make the collected information manageable.

The information can be collected in many different ways – as mentioned in previous chapters. There are data that in themselves provide information with a minimum of processing, such as the amount spent by a customer, the number of purchases, the time of purchase, and in the case of business to business who places the orders and size of annual purchases, etc.

Most companies also have access to data that with some processing and analysis can be converted to useful information. The pattern of purchases can tell a story. Is there seasonality? Is it many small purchases or a couple of big ones? What is the product mix? What does the type of product say about the customers' wants, needs and desires? While an inexperienced analyst will have to spend days or even months, people with experience, knowing what to look for, with the experience to make assumptions, approximations and conclusions can quickly come up with genuine insights. In one case an experienced team came up with genuine insights on the basis of only 2 days' analysis of a retailer's customer data.

A third way is to collect external information. Databases such as Mosaic and Acorn can provide additional insights into the customer as well as potential customer universes. There are also other sources. If a company is about to enter a new market sector, by observing what competitors are doing it is possible to form an initial view of the potential customers' behaviour.

For a company with its own direct financial relation to the customer, such as an electricity supplier, bank or telephone company, the collection of data is fairly easy even though at times it can be surprisingly difficult to make collected data accessible and usable. IT and invoicing systems are rarely built to generate customer insight but to provide correct accountancy, manufacturing and logistics information. Brand management information for customer insights requires, as mentioned previously, a very different perspective: less than 100% accuracy and more customer-centred structures.

For other companies there are other methods. Airlines have frequent flyer programmes, which track the behaviour of key customers. British Airways track its 600,000 to 700,000 most important customers with its Airmiles card and takes extra care and attention of the 40,000 or so Gold and Platinum card holders. Many retailers have card-based programmes to collect information. The customer shows the card, points are allocated to the card, the customer gets a reward and the company gets information.

> The master of the retail card is Tesco with its Clubcard. The Clubcard is not a unique programme in any way. Just like any other so-called loyalty card, you get a reward for shopping (in Tesco's case 1% of purchases) and a set of promotional offers to encourage you to come again, shop more, etc. When you apply for a card you give your address and some life stage data. The rest of the customer profile is collected through measuring the behaviour of the cardholders. To make a scheme worthwhile it is of course important that the card is used. Tesco has a usage of around 80% of total turnover; that is, Tesco can identify who bought what, when and in what context for 80% of its turnover through approximately 8 million active cardholders/households (out of a total of 23 million in the UK). It can also determine share of wallet, purchasing behaviour over time (e.g. tracking the usage of a specific product) and a number of other dimensions.

The main 'trick' lies, though, not in the skills to collect the information but to use it to understand customers for segmentation and in the case of a retailer for merchandising, pricing, ranging and all other aspects of retailing to be able to run a 'better store'.

The tool to do this is segmentation. How the segmentation is done depends of course on the circumstances, as described earlier. In the case of Tesco it is a sophisticated model with several levels; in many other cases it is a simple one-dimensional approach.

Traditionally customer data was collected through market research. You asked people what they had done, wanted to do and what they thought about it. In many cases not a very precise method as people do not always remember, may not like to tell the truth and it is very difficult cost-effectively to get hold of enough of a sample to be able to draw reasonably reliable conclusions. For consumer goods companies, sources like store audits (usually by AC Nielsen) provide information (but still based on a statistically limited sample); consumer panels are another source. These sources are less robust than the data collected at the point of purchase because there is no need to rely on people's memories, the purchasing data cover everything.

Not all businesses have nor need such advanced systems to start to gain better customer understanding.

A company we worked with had for many years focused on a particular age group in the sector where it was active. The company had also started to experience some stagnation in sales. The conclusion from a strategic review was that the original age group was saturated, no more business was to be had unless major investments were made, and that it 'must be' better to focus on a younger segment of the market. The company in question had collected the age of each customer so it was easy to establish how old the customers were. Indeed, the numbers showed, as expected, that the majority were in a certain age band.

What the company had not done, but we did, was to compare the numbers in each age band with the total target audience. The highest penetration in one age band was 8%, far away from saturation. Rather than trying to gain market share in another age band, unlikely to be easy as the brand was highly identified with its core market, our advice was to go for an increasing share of the core market. Eight per cent was far from the limit and most certainly it would be easier to go from 8% to 10% in the core market than from 0.5% to 2.5% in a non-core area. Two numbers alone, one from the company's own data and one from official statistics, were enough to change the company's growth strategy for the better. This example also illustrates the power of the Big Number: 8%.

Data can be a very powerful driver of your business, if used for understanding the customers better.

DESIRE? PROFITS?

To be able to build a more desirable brand, it is essential to understand the customers fully. How else can anyone know what to do to create a desirable proposition? Customer understanding is the key underlying element of customized brand propositions. By knowing who the best customers are, the ones generating a disproportionally high share of turnover, it is possible to focus on this group to ensure continued prosperity.

10
Step 3: know thyself

The purpose of this chapter is to explain why it is important to understand where the brand actually comes from. What is special about the product and the company? What is the company particularly good at?

WHERE ARE YOU COMING FROM? – THE PRODUCT

Long-surviving brands are built on a solid promise delivered by a product and/or service. McDonald's is the world's biggest restaurant chain not because of Ronald McDonald, but because McDonald's always delivers a consistent value-for-money product. Coca-Cola is the world's biggest soft drink brand not because children in the commercials once sang that 'we like to teach the world to sing', but because it is a refreshing drink with a very acceptable taste. A local restaurant will not get regular customers unless it serves good food and provides pleasant service, no matter how attractive the fascia is.

To be able to define and understand the offer of the brand correctly, it is important to grasp fully all the dimensions of the product or service. What is it that is special about the product? Unless this is perfectly clear to all, it is almost impossible to build a strong brand, let alone to customize the brand.

Our experience is that this is not as easy as it may seem. On numerous consultancy projects the questions 'What do you provide?' and 'What is so special about it?' have been answered in a superficial way. 'We make good quality products' or 'Our product is about the same as everyone else's' are common answers. Once, working with a food product, it was so difficult to get a reasonable answer from the brand management team that we immediately organized a full tasting session with all the competitive products to demonstrate to the team that there really was a difference between the brands.

People are not stupid and neither are customers. They do not choose a product or service without a reason. Although suppliers may believe they have an excellent product, customers may choose it because 'it is the cheapest' or 'it is the only one my distributor carries' or even 'it is the only name I can remember'. It can of course also be 'I really like to deal with these people' or 'what they deliver is really superb because . . .'. To understand why a product is chosen is very important, otherwise it is impossible to understand the brand. It is also not possible to develop the product proposition, nor adapt it to each brand proposition (see Step 4) as it is impossible to know what to improve without knowing where to start.

Not so long ago it was easy to explain why one product of one brand was superior to another. But that is no longer the case. There are very few market sectors where the competition is 'bad', they are all more or less good. When I first worked in the food industry in the 1970s many competitive products were close to being inedible – especially when it came to prepared convenience food. Just 10 years later almost all were perfectly acceptable – perhaps not excellent but totally adequate. As the differences between different brands in the vast majority of markets are so tiny it becomes even more important to identify those differences, so whatever competitive benefit is at hand can be understood, enhanced and exploited to grow the brand.

Once the reasons for buying are understood, that information can then be used as the basis for the next step of understanding why. What product parameters generate the positive, or negative, response? Is it the outstanding distribution system? Above average service and very quick turnaround rates for orders? Or superb performance in some other respect?

The answers to all these questions are rarely what first comes to mind. It requires probing internal experts and making external sources, asking customers and making competitive evaluations of products and services.

Understand the product – otherwise you will not be able to understand the customer and deliver something better.

WHERE ARE YOU COMING FROM? – THE COMPANY

Product features are not the result of magic but hard work in a company. Just as a customer does not buy a product without a reason, a company will not produce this product or service without some core skills. The core skills are usually an effect of historic development. Over time the organization has developed certain skills which it may or, more often than not, may not be aware of.

A core skill at BMW is to make exciting cars and motorbikes. A core skill at Sony is to develop new, home electronic products. A core skill at Nestlé and Unilever is to market consumer goods, nothing particularly unique, but they do it very well.

For successful brand management, these core skills, core capabilities, must be identified. The reason is that without knowing what the company is good at, it becomes a hit and miss affair to develop the brand. One organization we worked with thought they were very good at innovation. In reality they were no good at all at this, but very good at distributing a particular set of products. By changing the focus from trying to innovate to utilizing distribution strengths, the performance of the organization improved considerably.

Scandinavian Airlines once thought they were very good at delivering everything needed for a business person's travels so they bought hotels, travel agencies, invested in car rentals, etc. As history has shown Scandinavian Airlines were not particularly good at running these services and had to divest a number of the acquired companies. Making the Scandinavian Airlines brand stand for more than 'just' a Scandinavian Airline was a mistake, as the company could not deliver a competitive service. The brand did not gain any strengths from the exercise, and weakened instead.

Ryanair is another airline example where a core competence has been developed to underpin the promise of a low-cost airline. One key element of running an airline profitably is turnaround time. When the aircraft is on the ground, it does not generate revenue but costs money in the form of running costs, costs for using the airport, capital costs and depreciation charges. Ryanair has reduced the time the aircraft is on the ground. By not providing proper meals or newspapers, the aircraft does not have to wait for them to be taken on board. The clear-up of rubbish is done by the staff on board during the flight when passengers are asked to dump any rubbish in a bin carried around the cabin by the crew; passengers have to come early to the gate to make sure everyone gets on board quickly; there is no fixed seating (this is particularly clever because it does away with the cost of having a computer system to allocate the seats and it is an encouragement for all passengers to be at the gate early to get a good seat, thus ensuring no late passengers which could delay departure and cause problems at the other end), etc. By doing away with everything that extends the time on the ground Ryanair can turn around in 20 minutes, can afford to sell cheap tickets and has a core competence.

Most companies have a set of unique core skills. It is unusual that those skills are correctly defined. Many companies have vague statements about quality, teamwork, the building of value and the like, but these are not core capabilities, and they are certainly not anything that will lead to a unique competence to develop a differentiated brand. To define the core capabilities of the company producing the brand is an essential part of building the understanding part of the brand customization process. Without knowing what the company is good at, it is very difficult to develop the brand further.

Know the company's core capabilities – otherwise the brand will not be able to deliver, and continue to deliver, the promise

WHERE ARE YOU COMING FROM? – THE BRAND

The purpose of this book is not to describe how you build a brand. That subject was covered in my book *Competitive Branding* (John Wiley & Sons, 1998). This book is about customizing the brand to be even more competitive.

To customize the brand, the starting point is of course the current brand platform. A few paragraphs in a chapter is much too little space to cover the subject of developing a brand platform, but the text below is an attempt to cover some key aspects.

At its most basic a brand is the conceptualization of the reputation of a product, service, company, person or any other entity. That reputation is an effect of all the activities carried out under the brand name or brand symbol. What you feel and think about Coca-Cola is an effect of all the advertising, all the promotion, all the cans and bottles consumed (if any), all you have been told about the brand and all you have seen connected with the brand such as friends drinking it, sponsorship of sports events, etc.

The brand stands for a promise, a core positioning. Volvo is a safe car, Ferrari is a very fast and exciting car, Mercedes is a solid car, Coca-Cola is refreshing and so on. A clear positioning is essential for any brand but it is only the beginning. The positioning is like the bull's eye, the core and centre of the brand.

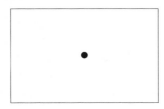

A brand carries certain values. Volvo is Swedish and reliable, Ferrari is Italian and macho, Mercedes is German and a status symbol, all further attributes of the brands mentioned above. Each brand has a set of brand values. Some are tied to tangible features such as 'crunchy' for a breakfast cereal or 'refreshing' for a soft drink. Others are tied to emotions such as 'honest' for a bank (we do trust them with our money so they better be) or 'traditional' for a lawyer. There are also brand values that are generic to a sector, such as 'good taste' for a food product, and there are those that are differentiating, such as 'racing tradition' for Jaguar cars.

Brand values are not the same as the culture of a company. Many mix the two. Culture can involve values such as teamwork, being innovative (even though the brand is not innovative) and being a responsible citizen in the local community. These are important in themselves but as management tools, they are not for brand development. The only link is that company culture values and brand values should harmonize, one should not be in opposition to the other. If the culture is traditional and old-fashioned it is difficult credibly and effectively to develop a brand that is hip and fashionable.

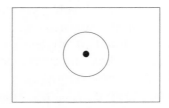

The brand values represent the layer outside the positioning. It is central to the brand but contains more dimensions than the positioning.

The next layer is the brand personality. We can say that the positioning is the heart, the values the body and the personality the clothes. Is this a lively brand or a boring one? Does it have sparkle? Or is it grey to fit into the world of reliability? Is it macho like many beer brands? Or all about steel and metal like BMW?

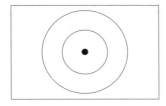

This overview of a brand platform is totally focused on the content of the brand as that is what is most important. A brand also usually has a symbol, its logo, and with it a visual identity and, ideally but not always, a defined copy identity. Many brands also have some brand properties (such as the Coke bottle and Marlboro red) that are important to retain and if appropriate develop.

It is of fundamental importance that the brand platform is defined prior to customizing the brand. The reasons should be obvious to all. If the core elements are not defined, it is impossible to know what to customize and to know whether it is being done the right or the wrong way?

Define the brand platform – and do it before going any further.

DESIRE? PROFITS?

The product, the company and the brand make up building blocks from which real desirability can be built.
Managing a brand can take up much time if not done effectively. By ensuring that all the building blocks are well defined prior to the customization process, the work will be quicker, better and less costly while still delivering an improved bottom line.

11
Step 4: customizing the brand proposition – the foundation for a truly desirable brand

The purpose of customizing the brand proposition is to bring it closer to the real life and world of the customer. Making it more relevant, more appropriate and, not least, making the brand more useful for the customer. In this chapter the process to achieve this is explored and explained.

The objective of the process is to develop a brand proposition, which for each customer will differentiate the brand in the mind of that particular customer (or potential customer) so that the brand will be perceived, experienced and accepted as superior and more desirable than other alternatives in the category.

To customize the brand is in one sense a totally straightforward process in that it is simply to adapt and adjust the brand proposition to the conditions of each individual customer. As explained earlier, that is the theory. The practical application of the theory is to adapt the brand proposition to each customer segment.

A FUNDAMENTAL REQUIREMENT: A WELL-DEFINED BRAND AND A SEGMENTATION MODEL

For a successful and effective customization process two things must be in place, a well-defined brand and a segmentation model.

First, unless the brand is properly defined it is, of course, impossible to customize it, as there will be nothing to customize. If the brand is not properly defined, defining it is the very first step, as highlighted in the previous chapter. However, even if it is defined it may well be advisable to go over the key elements again. There may be gaps in the definition. Are the brand values properly identified? Is the brand personality the real personality? Is the positioning correct? Was the brand definition carried out in brutal honesty or is it a wish list? Wish lists are not a good foundation for brand work so that in themselves they may be a reason for revisiting the brand definition. In my experience, there are in the vast majority of cases one or several good reasons for revisiting the brand definition prior to progressing the customization project. Not necessarily as a major project but to fill in the gaps and update it.

Second, to be able to customize the brand proposition, it is necessary to have developed a segmentation model. Whether there are 3 or 20 segments, or whether it is a 1 or 3-level segmentation model is in one sense neither here nor there – it all depends on the circumstances such as the market situation, the competitive situation and available data. What matters is whether the model is appropriate, whether it is practical to work with, that each segment is sufficiently different from the others (otherwise there is not much point in having a segmentation) and that there is enough information regarding each segment to be able to develop a fully customized brand proposition including customized products and services.

Without a brand definition and segmentation model, it is impossible to customize a brand.

COMPETITIVE CONTEXT

The conceptual starting point is the customer. It is for the customer's benefit that the brand is customized. It is to make the brand even more appealing to the individual customer that the brand is customized.

From a practical point of view, the first step is to identify the customers, which is why the segmentation model is so important. By splitting up the total target audience into different segments, the individual customer can be put into context and at the same time into a unit that is functional and practical to work with.

How you structure the customer understanding can have a fundamental impact on the end result. Traditionally the segmentation is based on tangible socio-economic information. More advanced segmentation uses lifestyle dimensions and attitudes (see previous chapters).

To differentiate a brand successfully the competitive context is of fundamental importance. This is simply logical. The customized brand has to be seen as different to the competitive ones in the minds of the customers in the segment. Consequently it is crucial to understand the competitive context of each segment.

This can be done in two different ways. Either the competitive context is the determining factor for the segmentation, complemented by other factors, or the segmentation model is developed from the customer behaviour perspective and then complemented by information regarding the competitive context. *If* the brand is in a market with well-defined distinct brands the first approach is not only a possibility but should also be the first alternative to be considered. However, if the market is full of brands that are bland and me-too's, the second alternative is the only practical model as the competitive brand scenario will not be good enough to form the basis of a segmentation model.

To summarize, the starting point for the customization process is to establish the competitive context per segment. The starting point is either the competitive context leading to a segmentation model or a segmentation model leading to a competitive context. Which way to work depends on the circumstances and the real solution, in the spirit of no black-and-white recommendations, may well be best to do both in parallel.

The competitive context and segmentation model form the foundation on which the customized brand proposition is built.

CUSTOMIZING THE BRAND PROPOSITION

This is the starting point of a process and a strategy that will take the brand to a higher level of customer acceptance and desirability. For each segment the brand proposition is customized to the specific requirements of each segment. Once the basic proposition has been defined for each segment, the different elements can be developed. What is a product/service package? The marketing mix? The marketing communication? The channels of distribution and pricing? What will the result be on the bottom line?

BMW is one of the best-managed brands in Europe, if not the world. Its consistent work over the last 30 years has led to a very strong position, a clear message as well as a distinct identity. All encapsulated in 'the ultimate driving machine'. The only challenge for the brand seems to be to keep it all on track and continue to develop.

While BMW at a quick glance does not seem to be customizing its brand, the reality is different. The tag line 'the ultimate driving machine' represents the overall brand proposition. This is a car for people who like driving. BMW is the car for people who think that the car in itself matters most. It is about machines, not people. The emotions sit in the metal, the engine, the driving.

But the ultimate driving machine experience is very different for a family of four or a single young male. Irrespective of whether the driver is a rich, successful businessperson or a middle manager or whether the car is for people who like motorway cruising, traditional sports cars or driving across rough terrain (or wants to give the impression of doing this), there is a BMW model. The family man might drive a 320 estate, the single young male a 320Ci Coupe, the businessperson an 840, the middle manager a 520, the motorway cruiser a 525, the sports car fan a Z3 and the off-road enthusiast the X5. The product, proposition, price point and message differ for each of these categories. The brand is customized within the framework of a well-defined brand.

To customize the brand is to tie together the brand proposition with each segment, making sure that what is offered is really what the individual would like to have at an affordable price and in a way that is appealing.

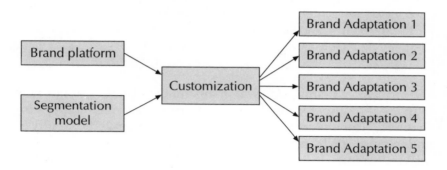

Dell's founder Michael Dell is someone who has fully grasped the power of a customized brand. In some ways the Dell proposition is utterly customized, in others less so.

The product and service package is in the Dell model totally customized as it is made to order. No need to even segment as each individual can get what he or she wants within the parameters of the Dell brand (and effectively the parts available at the Dell factories).

Communication, on the other hand, in respect of the consumer market, is not very selective nor segmented. Dell is, as far as we can understand, applying the principle of self-selection. The prospective customer takes in the information that is of interest and forgets about the rest. It is also a very product-led type of communication that is typical for a market sector that has still not, from a brand point of view, reached the mature stage where intangible values are required for success.

Interestingly Dell has a more developed segmentation model for the business market with a segmentation based primarily on size, because that is the relevant criterion for this type of market complemented, where appropriate, with type of business such as health care and federal government.

Michael Dell is definitely in the forefront when it comes to one particular type of communication, customer feedback. On more than one occasion he has stated that the customers who are the most important are those with views, not those who bring in the biggest orders. The reason is of course that by getting feedback the brand proposition can be improved which will make more customers more satisfied and generate much more business in the future.

The principles behind building a customized brand are not new, they are the same for any brand and are as described in previous chapters. The difference lies in the thinking and the ability to understand each individual segment for building a more relevant brand. A fundamental difference in philosophy as well as practice to the common approach of just tweaking the brand proposition for short-term tactical gains.

It is just as important for a customized brand as any other to ensure relevance, appropriateness and to develop an appealing proposition, but this must be considered for each segment. Each segmented brand proposition must be seen as sensible and under-standable, and not contrived, by all customers. It is not enough for it to make sense to the segment itself. All other segments must also accept it, otherwise the total brand proposition will fail.

The customized brand proposition is the starting point for all other activities, the whole marketing mix, so unless it is properly developed, the rest will not work.

Take great care, spend time and be creative in getting the brand proposition by segment right.

DON'T GO TOO FAR

There are dangers with running a customized brand – as with most things. The following describes how it is possible to avoid the main danger, which is to customize the brand too much.

It may seem strange to state in a book introducing the concept of customized branding that it can be over done. The reason is that at first glance it may seem ideal to customize each element of the marketing mix to each individual segment.

A theoretical example would be if BMW were to extend its range by also including a low-cost and low-performance car as an entry model. It may be a great, short-term business proposition but it would dilute the brand. It is highly likely that the buyers of the 'ultimate driving machine' would feel let down and be annoyed if a small, low-performance car with the same name as the one they are driving – and had paid 'good money' for – was put on the market.

Or, what would the perception be if BMW, in advertising the 3-series, decided to abandon the existing brand identity and started to show beautiful people, romance and the many other traditional clichés of car advertising because one part of the potential audience was responding to this? Such activities would destroy the brand appeal for loyal buyers of, say, a Z3, and the Z3 driver may choose another brand next time.

The reason for not going too far down the customization route is that individuals do not live in a vacuum. If the romantic BMW commercial was ever made and was only shown to those who were in the segment of romantic car buyers and these people were totally isolated from other BMW customers, or potential customers, it would be OK. It would still not be a good strategy because the economies of scale in brand building would disappear, but it would not be a disaster. However, individuals do not, fortunately, live isolated from each other, they communicate. This means that the brand has to be seen as a coherent unit. It must be a totality that makes sense. Although adapting to different situations and target groups does make sense, to be totally different depending on the situation does not.

Reason number one for avoiding total customization is that with such an approach the brand profile will suffer, as illustrated above. If the brand is totally customized, Customer *A* cannot talk to Customer *B* about the same brand because they will have different brand concepts in their minds. However, if the brand has been adapted to *A* and *B*, they can talk because the basis is the same brand concept although it has been adapted so that it is more relevant making both of them more enthusiastic.

Reason number two for avoiding total customization is that it does away with the benefits of mass communication. There are benefits to targeted communication because it is more appropriate to the individual's situation, but there are also great benefits to mass communication. If, for instance, word-of-mouth communication is to work, and it is one of the most cost-effective ways of communicating with customers, the brand story has to be consistent – otherwise there will be total confusion. Equally, different types of display advertising and PR require a consistent brand profile, otherwise it will not be cost-effective.

Don't go beyond common sense.

DON'T FORGET TO CO-ORDINATE

For a customized brand the requirements regarding co-ordination are greater than those of a traditional brand. Not only must all the elements of the company work in the same direction, the different activities building the brand, which can involve a great number of people, must lead to the same end result, a stronger brand.

An example highlighting this lack of co-ordination is an incident involving British Telecom, the telephone company, and our own households.

A couple of years ago British Telecom was heavily criticized for letting people run up telephone bills without knowing it. The real reasons were rarely found and resolved. BT often refused to admit that mistakes had been made and the customers refused to pay, as they claimed they had not been in the house at the time of the calls. As a service to this segment of the market, BT introduced a 'watching brief' concept which meant that if the pattern of calls on a certain telephone line changed dramatically it would call the number in question and check whether this was OK. At face value a good idea.

At the same time, BT also introduced a customer service system to encourage more calls and show people who used the phone a lot that BT appreciated this – classical loyalty marketing technique. But the two activities were not co-ordinated.

In December–January 2000, my family had to make a number of telephone calls to Sweden, each one lasting about 30 minutes. Of course, the phone bill increased dramatically, understandably. Shortly after this we received a phone call from someone at BT who rather aggressively questioned the call pattern – as if investigating a fraud: Who had made the calls? Were we aware of these calls? Would we like to pay the bill in instalments, etc. This resulted in a lot of family tension, and, to put it mildly, we did not appreciate this service. It was 'Big Brother' watching and interfering. Some BT brand values quickly diminished in our minds.

A published case was even more dramatic. This involved someone who was carrying out market research, sending faxes with questions to radio stations around the globe as part of a major project. The faxes went off, increasing the phone bill dramatically. The faxes included a response mechanism so that the answers could be faxed back. After having sent out the faxes, the individual went on holiday expecting the fax machine to be full of responses on his return. Not so. The unexpected use of the telephone line meant a phone call from BT to enquire. No one answered – the person involved had gone on a well-deserved holiday. BT cut off the phone line, as it did not receive an explanation, so the answers to the questionnaires could not get faxed back. All that BT achieved was ill will from the person and ill will through the publicity that ensued, showing itself as an uncaring, insensitive company.

The final straw was the mailing to our household a couple of weeks later from BT. In the letter we were thanked for being such a good customer. The letter was presumably being triggered by the same system that started the enquiry process. There were two parts of a company not knowing what the other one did with the same customer being segmented in two different ways: first, as a suspected

> criminal using the phone too much and, second, as a high-value customer whom BT would like to thank to get us to use the phone even more.

Don't customize beyond your capabilities.

KEEP IT TOGETHER

To keep the brand together as one brand two things are important:

1 The brand needs to be properly defined. This is always important but more so when it comes to customized brands as the strain on the brand is greater and the opportunities to go off the rails are more frequent. The brand and the adaptations have to be tightly controlled at all times.
2 The overall brand platform must be implemented not only on paper but in the hearts and minds of all in the customer interface. Everyone must know what to do. It is to expect too much that everybody will know what segment a customer belongs to, but as long as the overall brand platform is totally and properly understood things are unlikely to go wrong.

Define the brand, and keep the brand discipline.

IF ONLY DOING PART OF THE JOB?

A common first step to a proper customized brand is to individualize part of the marketing mix. Communication may be customized while product delivery is not. Campaign promise is customized but the overall promise remains the same. Different product variants, in effect customized, and similar brand profile. Many car brands take this approach.

While such a business would be more successful with a fully customized programme, it is a first start. However, there are still the inherent dangers of splitting the brand profile. The need for

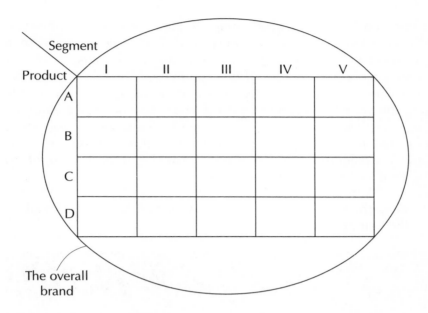

tight management, knowing what the brand stands for and how to adapt it, remains crucial. If going too far, as in the fictitious BMW example above, the brand will be damaged.

No matter what the level of customization is, the brand must be well defined and held together.

INDIVIDUALIZED YET FROM ONE SUPPLIER

One major challenge is to ensure that all customers perceive all the offers to come from the same supplier, that it makes sense that this supplier is offering all these different alternatives and, ideally, that its ability to do so becomes a strength rather than something that is diluting the brand equity.

This challenge is not new. It was the same for suppliers during previous periods of customization, such as the furniture makers of the 18th century. The challenge was, and is, to ensure that each individual customer feels recognized and respected while ensuring that there is a common reputation built around key values and a strong positioning. If that common denominator does not exist, it is not a brand. And, if it is not a brand, one person can't recommend a supplier to another because of lack of confidence in the abilities of this company.

The more the target audience is split up into different segments and the more the segments differ in characteristics, the greater the need and temptation to customize. Consequently the more essential it is that the common denominators are well defined and consistently used to ensure that the brand is built to become as strong a brand as possible.

Keep the balance between the customized propositions and the main one.

DESIRE? PROFITS?

A more relevant brand is a more desirable brand and a desirable brand is one where all parts of the marketing mix make sense to all segments.
A more desirable brand is a more profitable brand if it is managed properly.

12

Step 5: the foundation for sustainable desirability: the product/service package

At the very heart of a strong brand sits the product/service package. This is what the customer is buying. A product, a service or, more and more, a total package. With a new car you get a service package. If a company buys a machine, it comes with installation, training for employees and service guarantee in case something goes wrong.

The origins of branding go back to the need to identify a product, who actually had made the product so that the prospective customer could form an opinion as to the quality. This has not changed. While the intangible benefits of a brand are increasingly important, that does not diminish the need for a strong product/ service package. Even the strongest brand can run into problems if quality is below expectations – as Levi's experienced in the 1970s – or if product development is lagging behind – as Ericsson in recent years has experienced in its competitive struggle with Nokia in the market for mobile phones.

Unless a company gets the product/service package 'right', there is no future for the brand. No matter how clever or appealing a communication strategy may be, if the product or service does not deliver on the promise, the brand has no future. Even though it is true that no one will beat a path to your door just because you have built a better mousetrap – you have to tell the world about it – it is equally true that no one will come unless there is a better mousetrap on offer. That is why this tangible aspect of the brand proposition comes first among the different chapters covering the marketing mix.

The purpose of this chapter is to explore some of the issues relating to customizing the product/service offer of the brand proposition.

The customised brand approach does open up two different avenues for making the product better. The first one is that with a brand strategy based on individual attention information is collected on an individual basis, and from that it is possible to reach conclusions based on real customer insights which can be used to develop a better product. Second, and a more obvious one, is that by adapting the offer to different customer segments the product will be much more appropriate and consequently, everything else being equal, perceived as better value.

MAKING A BETTER PACKAGE

It is an axiom to say that with better information you can develop better and more appropriate products. This can, though, take different formats.

> Tesco, the UK retailer and master of customer information, used its 8 million customer database as a fountain of information when developing the Tesco 'finest' range. A range of superior, quality-food products aimed at taking the high ground in food retailing – a position previously held by Marks & Spencer. Understanding the customers meant that the right products could be developed and the end result was a highly successful launch.

Customer information in more traditional industries is of course also useful. Customer insight is, as all experienced marketing executives know, the driver behind good marketing and, in particular, when it comes to developing the offer.

A by-now classical example is that of Nestlé UK in the late 1970s and early 1980s, when the simple but crucial insight that key customer groups were reducing the amount of milk used for coffee led to a change of strategy. Less milk in a cup of coffee means that the quality of the coffee becomes more important.

Consequently, to increase the acceptance of their coffee, better beans were required. Better beans are of course more expensive but fortunately for Nestlé this coincided with a dramatic fall in coffee prices, which meant that the quality could be increased without an increase in selling price. An insight which formed the foundation for the strength of the brand over the following 15–20 years.

Traditionally, product improvements and development of new products have been based on a combination of analysis of market trends and creativity/intuition. The combination of the two will always be required, but the advantages gained by better customer insights mean that mistakes can to a greater extent be avoided and that creativity and inspiration can take place against a backdrop of real customer information rather than qualified guesswork as so often in the past.

Use customer information to build a better mousetrap.

IMPACT ON THE PRODUCT
DEVELOPMENT STRATEGY

For a brand to succeed in the longer term it needs to reinvent its offer constantly, adding value to the brand through improvements in all aspects of the market mix. Constant improvement is crucial to a successful competitive strategy. The rationale and techniques to achieve this are described in my previous books *Value-Added Marketing* (McGraw-Hill, 1992) and *Competitive Branding* (John Wiley & Sons, 1998).

Product development is either New Product Development (NPD) or Old Product Development (OPD) (the OPD concept was introduced in *Value-Added Marketing*). Customizing the brand will of course impact both types of activity but the latter more than the former.

NPD will improve due to better customer insight and the ability to test new products on selected target groups. The effects of better customer insights have been described above and the application to NPD is actually nothing new. The need remains, though. New products and brands continue to have failure rates of 90% or so for most companies; generating better customer insight to improve the success rate can be a highly profitable activity.

A segmented view of the target market makes it easier to manage a gradual introduction of a new concept. It is often not necessary, or even advisable, to launch a new service to all customers. It can be appropriate to start with one segment, or even subsegment, and then develop and adapt as more segments are included. For instance, in financial services it is possible to select who to target with a new credit card offer, measure the response in the different subsectors, perhaps add extra market research, refine the offer and in due course adapt the offer to each segment, one by one.

The big change will come, though, in resources and applications required for OPD. The whole process of adapting products and services to different segments requires OPD techniques. These essential activities to adapt and improve the product include understanding the requirements, improving and adapting to the different needs of the different segments and picking up signals from the target groups to make the offer even better. This should also include monitoring the development in each segment to see whether learning from one segment can be transferred to another.

As mentioned above, most brands offer not a product nor a service but a combination of the two. For segmented OPD this is very important as it opens up more variables for customizing the offer. It may in many cases be much more efficient to offer a similar or even identical physical product, but to customize the service package totally. Different individuals, or companies, may have different requirements regarding reassurance, financial risk, worries about breakdowns, instructions and training, etc. making such a strategy highly attractive.

OPD is, however, not only about adapting to the needs of the segments and constantly improving the offer. A necessary pre-requisite for a successful brand is an efficient operation so that the brand is profitable. An essential part of OPD is to ensure that the product and service is produced efficiently.

> The original rationale behind McDonald's was low-cost pro-duction – that was the focus of the McDonald brothers in San Bernardino when they built the first McDonald hamburger restaurant. The low costs allowed them to sell burgers cheaper than anyone else providing superior value for money.

> IKEA drives down costs on all products with enormous energy. Items like moulded plastic furniture have been reduced in price by a factor of more than 5 and at the same time improved in quality – no doubt leading to much higher sales. A superb example of OPD and achieving true value for money.

> Banks are in a fairly unique position in that they have detailed access to customer information. Most banks do not use this to their advantage. However, one European bank used customer data to construct not only a highly efficient customer contact programme but used the same information to launch new services as well, such as new types of bank account combining savings and borrowing with innovative features.

Customer insight is a great driver of more successful NPD and OPD.

MAXIMIZE CUSTOMIZATION FOR THE CUSTOMER, MINIMIZE IT FOR THE COMPANY

The brand perception is not formed at the desk of the product designer but in the minds of the customers. For best brand building effect, customization should be maximized in the minds of the customers, not in the factory or at service delivery. The more the customer feels that 'this is specially made for me' the better, and the more this can be achieved with minimal costs, the better. However, the adaptations have to be real. Badge marketing, as discussed earlier, is not the way forward any more.

A classical and traditional way of customizing is to put a monogram on a shirt. The same type of shirt could have different monograms. Certainly individualized. The monogram idea is, though, not out of fashion. It is possible to get an individualized word stitched on a pair of Nike trainers.

On a totally different level, every truck is still customized to the buyer's requirements. And almost every new car is to a larger or lesser degree customized as well. The colour, the trim, the size and type of engine, 'extras' such as radio and navigation systems, etc. all add up to a great number of variants.

But, and an important but, as described in the chapter on segmentation, the cost of adapting to the segments must always result in revenue that exceeds the total cost of adaptation. If not, it is better to offer the 'standard' product and find other ways of customizing the brand.

First, this means that each customization element has to be evaluated from a cost–benefit point of view. Second, each activity should be ranked from a cost–benefit point of view. Third, those elements and activities that cost less and generate most customization effect should be selected. For the motor industry, the customization can have an additional cost of close to zero as it is fed into the production system. In reality, in most cases there is probably a profit opportunity in the 'extras' as the margin is relatively higher on the extra features than on the basic car.

All this leads to a trade-off between individualization, customization, segmentation and the true mass-market approach of one-size-fits-all. Each market is different and it is impossible to state that one alternative is better than another. What is possible to state, however, is the trend. To be able to compete in the future, more and more customization will be required, for reasons explained elsewhere in the book. The strategic decision is when to start active customization – rather than reactive – or just doing it when required by customers to be able to get an order, or deciding that one-size-fits-all is the strategy and take the consequences. In the vast majority of cases the former is to be preferred, at least if the business objectives include building a strong brand – but not always.

> Aldi in Germany is an exception and follows the one-size-fits-all strategy. The range choice in an Aldi discount store in Germany is limited to a fraction of that of a traditional, large supermarket. There is no desire to customize the offer. A 'take it or leave it' attitude is behind the brand. Aldi is very successful and has in particular in Germany, its home market, a strong following as people have learnt to accept and even love the low prices and limited choice.
>
> In other markets it has been less successful as the segment accepting the Aldi trading style is smaller and the point of difference is less pronounced.

In most markets and for most brands the trend toward customization is inevitable. This has implications for how products and services are produced. The forward-looking company tackles this head-on and drives the process in a direction suitable for the company rather than waiting for the competition to take the initiative and then be left behind.

Please the customers with minimum efforts.

HOW TO DO IT

The obvious way of customizing is to produce and deliver a product suitable to the individual. The less obvious, but almost equally effective, is to let the customer do the selection. Which way to do it depends on the market dynamics, the way that trade is carried out.

> Direct banking is an example of total customization. Each customer can be offered a specific set of products and services. However, to offer a customer 200 different savings products does not make sense. It causes total confusion in the minds of the customers. Choosing between 20 different alternatives for pension investments can be difficult enough. The company that wants to build a customized brand selects what ought to be appropriate based on available knowledge, say 10 different alternatives, explains why these have been selected and perhaps offers a few not so obvious choices as a guarantee against getting the segmentation and choice of products wrong. Twelve alternatives rather than 200.

This as an example is ideal, but not all businesses can be run that way. Retailing is one example. It is not practically feasible to have ten different supermarkets or department stores in the same location. The strategy to adapt is to make sure that each shop has enough choice to fulfil the requirements of the customers. Segmenting the shop's target group, adapting the range to the profile and ensuring that all reasonable alternatives are available will be sufficient for customizing the brand's product/service package, especially if complemented with online, telephone or mailed services which are directly customized.

The need to serve an increasingly differentiated target audience is at least part of the reason for the continuing increase in the number of items stocked by most retailers. As mentioned earlier, the large, UK grocery retailers Tesco and Sainsbury have in their larger units over 25,000 different items, 30 years ago Sainsbury's stocked 4,000.

> Pick-and-mix sweetshops, particularly successful in Sweden, represent one type of retailing that is representative of this thinking. The shops are fairly small and only sell sweets.

Virtually the full range is pick-and-mix, there is a unit price per 100 g, sometimes there is a basic and a premium price and the choice is extensive with 100–150 different alternatives to choose from. A successful formula of non-customized pricing and self-selective range providing a very customized service.

The T-range concept is a useful strategy for any brand with a range. We first introduced the T-range for a cheese producer as a way to illustrate an effective range strategy.

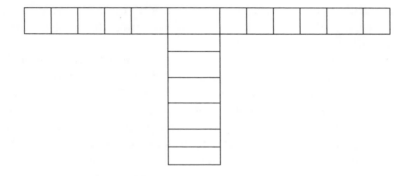

Each range of products has a couple of items that form the basis of the business, that have wide acceptance and are something 'all' customers expect the supplier to offer. For such products the supplier needs to offer a wide choice, many variants, in short a subrange with depth. This is illustrated by the stem of the T. In this figure it is a single product, but it can of course be two or more. This is usually the part of the range where there is price awareness and price competition as well.

To give the range profile, and to be able to offer each individual customer what he or she would like to have, it is necessary to have a choice, a selection of alternative products. These may have limited appeal to the majority, but for many individuals they are a required item. In addition, these products build the profile of the range and consequently the brand. If the brand profile is one of 'sport', the brand must offer many different types of 'sport' product even if they may not sell many. A jewellery shop 'must have' some exclusive diamond items even though the actual sales are limited. The wine lists of high-quality restaurants must have very expensive wines listed even though they rarely sell any.

The bar of the T illustrates these products. A wide range to build the profile, but not much depth is required as the purpose is to illustrate a certain concept/style and turnover per item is probably low.

With a T-range product strategy the brand will have the foundations for a self-selecting, customized range strategy. If the range is not self-selecting but each customer is provided with a choice, the thinking still applies, but then the T needs to be customized for each segment and of course will be much smaller. However, in most cases, that means, when it is all summed up, that the total range will still look like a T.

The self-selecting range strategy is the easiest to manage of the two alternative range strategies, but it does put part of the strategy in the hands of the customers and it only works where it is possible for the customer to get an overview. In a supermarket this is possible, likewise in a well-structured catalogue such as those published by wholesalers to businesses. It is also possible for internet-based companies such as Amazon.com.

In many digital, consumer products the customization is left totally to the customer. The seller provides a menu of alternatives from which you can configure your own product. The reason is that it is relatively cheap to add extra features. This can lead to a less distinct brand as one part of the marketing mix is taken out of the brand building tool mix unless the process to self-select is made particularly relevant, such as ease of use for the buyer.

If the supplier has the opportunity to pre-select, like a financial services or a mail order company, the decision-making process will be simplified for the customer and the number of choices available have no practical limitations. It is not difficult to supply a bicycle in 11,000 variants or a car in 17,000 (a BMW Z3 roadster), as the item is made to order. At the other end of the spectrum, such as preparing a proposal for a consultancy project to a large company, the variants are almost infinite. There are so many different ways within the framework of the promise, the brand proposition, to deliver the product that it is almost impossible to count them all. From a sales point of view, though, the more and better customized the proposition is from the beginning, the more likely it is that the customer will accept the proposal.

Since the mid-1990s many experiments among consumer goods companies have taken place to offer more customized products. Many of these have failed, often due to that fact that the product strategy has not been a part of a coherent customized branding strategy, while others have succeeded.

Levi's was a pioneer in this field and already in 1996 offered bespoke items with a direct link to the factory. Levi's has since developed several other concepts, including getting your jeans fitted with special features and designs.

General Mills in the USA ran an experiment with customizing breakfast cereals. The consumers could order a specially made product, customized not only by taste but also health profile. The initiative failed – perhaps not surprisingly given the portion price of $1.

Procter & Gamble runs an online service with personalized beauty products under the brand Reflect.com. With the help of online services, the consumer gets individual advice and tailor-made products customized to fit the consumer's skin type and colour scheme. Information regarding the level of success is not available to the author but the site is in existence at the time of writing, which is a sign of success.

While consumers no doubt appreciate customized products, they are only prepared to buy if it is convenient, relevant and value for money – just like any other product.

Suggesting and delivering a customized product is the established way of working in some market sectors, such as project management, building contractors and large investments for factories. Other sectors rely almost totally on self-selection by the customer. This category includes many retailers, restaurants and catalogue-based (whether paper or digital) businesses. There is of course also a large middle sector, such as cars, where the product is customized within a set and fairly limited framework in the sales process between the salesperson and the customer.

To take customization one step further in order to make a brand a leader in customized branding requires, at least, two things, customer information and production flexibility. By understanding the customers it is possible to come up with suggestions which will not only fulfil but also exceed the expectations of the customer. Flexibility in delivering the product or service is the other side of the process. If the company has a rigid structure, it will not be possible to deliver the customized product and the brand will be better off, at least in the short term, by sticking to the traditional 'one size fits all'. That is, though, not an advisable option in most cases, and, as most companies already today have some sort of flexibility, the challenge is to improve flexibility and make it a combative tool for marketing while maintaining profitability.

Customize the offer but do it in a way appropriate to the market segment.

DESIRE? PROFITS?

Without a product/service package that is appropriate to the customer, there will not be any desire to buy. Using customer information to develop and enhance the offer is the first step, the second is to customize the offer to each market segment. How to do this depends on the market circumstances, from a totally customized process to self-selection by the customer.

The profit challenge is twofold. First, as with any product development issue, the enhancement in customer appeal must take into account the cost of making the product or delivering the service. It should ideally be cheaper, not more expensive. Second, to customize can easily become expensive if the process is not managed carefully. More variants can lead to increases in stockholding, shorter production runs, retraining of staff, etc. Building flexibility into the process and managing how the customized product is delivered is important, as the customized brand will not be successful unless the additional margin from the customization process is higher than the costs for doing it.

13
Step 6: getting into the customers' hands

It is a 'motherhood statement' to say that if the customer can't get the product or service, it is highly unlikely there will be a sale. All marketing efforts will come to nothing if the customers can't get the product or experience the service. Some companies distribute directly to the final customer, others use different types of middleman, such as retailers and wholesalers. Service delivery can also be made in many different ways, such as face-to-face, electronically or by post.

Yet, the majority of marketing executives, in our experience, do not take the issue of distribution, the physical supply, seriously. The purpose of this chapter is to illustrate the importance of distribution as a part of a customized brand proposition.

CONSIDER THE OPTIONS

Distribution has in many companies an off-centre role. Production and sales are seen as important, how to get the product from *A* to *B*, that is, 'something someone somewhere will take care of'. In many cases the actual physical distribution may well be out-sourced for good reasons, but where to deliver and how remains a key part of the customized brand strategy for reasons mentioned in the Introduction.

In most markets different segments prefer to get delivery in different ways. If the approach is mass-market, there is but one way – the most cost-effective. If a customized approach is taken, the cost-effectiveness has to be considered from a broader perspective, perhaps the customer is prepared to pay more for a different delivery method.

The Coca-Cola Company is by many, the author included, considered as one of the best when it comes to physical distribution. The achievement of being the first delivery lorry into East Berlin when the Wall came down was not a quirk but the result of a long-term strategy going back, at least, to World War II. At the time the USA entered the war, a claim or promise was made that each GI should have a Coca-Cola within 'arm's reach'. To deliver on that promise meant going across the globe – and Coca-Cola did.

A most interesting aspect of Coca-Cola, nowadays, from a marketing – distribution perspective is the link between pricing and distribution. Buying a 2-litre bottle of Coke in Safeway's costs £1.35 (£0.67/litre) and to buy a 50-cl bottle in the same supermarket is £0.79 (£1.58/litre). To buy a 33-cl can in a sandwich shop is £0.75 (£2.25/litre). To buy a glass of Coke in a pub is around £1.00 (around £5.00/litre) and to buy a glass in a restaurant can cost £2.50 (£17.50/litre). While the service content varies considerably in each case, the price differentials are also considerable. And, it is worth noting that with the possible exception of the pub prices (in comparison with alcoholic drinks), the different prices are seen to be perfectly acceptable because they make sense to the final consumer. Although we do not have any access to any pricing information from the Coca-Cola Company it is probably fair to assume that the profit for the supplying company in relative terms increases in a similar way to the price per litre – although not to the same extent.

It is also fair to assume that the main reason for utilizing all these distribution channels, and many more, is to gain total market coverage. Reaching every segment of the market, wherever it may be. The message may not be particularly customized but the distribution certainly is. Many more companies could learn a lot from this aggressive policy and gain considerable market share in the process – in our view.

Just by considering the options, many companies will gain an advantage as, subjectively, distribution is one of the last remaining bastions of the blinkered application of physical economies of scale. As illustrated above with Coca-Cola, the most efficient distribution system, large lorries to a large hypermarket, is not necessarily the most profitable for the company and certainly not the way to reach all customer segments on all possible consumption occasions.

The choice of channels can also change over time.

The IKEA company started out over 50 years ago as a mail order company in the south of Sweden. In 1965, after about 15 years, it opened the first big out-of-town store in Stockholm. After another couple of years, the company expanded abroad where it rarely used mail order as a distribution technique.

With the advent of the Internet, direct delivery is back on the agenda and IKEA is now, in many countries, running a website with a virtual store where you can buy products and get them delivered straight to your home.

Looking at each customer segment and considering how to reach the various parts of the target audience will force a reconsideration of distribution methods. The conclusion may well be that the existing methods are fine, but to neglect the issue can be costly. What are the alternatives? What does the competition do? Will a middleman, such as a wholesaler, do a better job than in-house? During the transition in the UK grocery market from manufacturer distribution to retailer distribution, many companies, including Findus UK, used wholesalers to cover the smaller shops once the big shops had established their own systems and the manufacturer could no longer afford to run its own distribution network.

Make sure all options are explored – a customer will only buy what is easily available.

A BRAND MARKETING-LED DISTRIBUTION STRATEGY

By considering the options from a marketing, and in particular customized branding, point of view, a company may well conclude that it needs to expand its distribution methods or to manage the existing portfolio in a more active way.

Most successful companies work with a main distribution channel and then supplement this with other ways of reaching all segments. In the Coca-Cola case the Coca-Cola fleet of vehicles is usually the main channel. In the IKEA case the store is the main channel.

The most sensible approach is to review the main customer segments, look at how they should get the product and then build this channel into the main channel, making it as cost-effective as possible while still maintaining appropriate service levels. Then add on other channels to ensure as complete a coverage as possible. If one channel is more expensive than another, pricing has to reflect this unless there are good strategic reasons not to. The customer can then make a choice based on available facts.

The distribution system comes under particular pressure at times of change. It may not be possible to dismantle an old system while having to build a new one in parallel. Banks are such examples.

Banks used to do all their business over the counter. The customers came in during limited opening hours, queued up and did whatever was required in face-to-face contact with the clerk behind the desk. Expensive, of course, but easy to manage: 'one size fits all'.

> Then came mail-based payment systems, ATMs for drawing cash, ATMs with payment and money transfer features, telephone banking, Internet banking, banking at the grocery check-out, and perhaps a few more. But, bank counters are still needed as are other forms of personal service.

Some banks saw some of these new systems as a way of saving money – taking the accountant's view – rather than as a way to give better service and, if there was any savings, share the rewards with the customers. If a customer is doing part of the job the clerk used to do – and especially if the local branch has been closed as an effect of this – the customer expects to get a cheaper service as a reward for his or her work. The brand perspective is to see it as a way of, first, providing better service to defined customer categories and, second, if savings are made, sharing those with the customers so that there is a feeling of mutual benefit that will build brand appreciation and customer loyalty.

Technology has meant that distribution systems have exploded into a multitude of channels. But many banks are now at a loss to choose the main channel. What is to drive the distribution system? The branches or the Internet? What are the requirements of the different segments? Does the brand proposition deliver across the channels? Many questions need to be settled if a bank is to build a distinct and differentiating distribution strategy that will end up supporting a relevant, customized brand proposition.

Knowing where to distribute a brand can make or break the concept.

> An example that illustrates the need for integrating the distribution strategy and the brand strategy is Puma. Puma is a German sportswear company with a range of sports shoes (specializing in trainers), originally a sister company to the more famous Adidas, that went through a number of changes in management and ownership in the 1980s and 1990s and ended up with a muddled brand image. By

segmenting the customer base into appropriate categories, then using distinct distribution channels for each category and thus getting rub-off effect on the brand proposition, the company has rebuilt its position. Luxury sportswear was put in luxury stores, specialist goods for BMX and skateboarding was put in specialist shops and fashion accessories in designer shops. A customized brand strategy materialized, primarily driven by the distribution channels.

The other part of the strategy was to get out of inappropriate channels, such as JCPenneys and K-mart in the USA. Many companies are happy to increase distribution channels, especially when going upmarket. The other side of the coin, to have to exit unsuitable distribution channels, a necessity for a credible strategy, is for many harder. However, credibility will disappear if consistency is not honoured as the totality must form a coherent unit. Puma did do it and has so far reaped the rewards in increasing sales and earnings.

For many brands the distribution channel is an integral part of the brand perception, like Puma's. If a brand is seen in the 'right' places, it makes sense to all segments. If seen in the wrong places, people get confused and the brand perception suffers.

Most brands require a variety of distribution channels to ensure that each main customer segment actually gets the product or service in the best possible way. The advice is that these possibilities need to be reviewed from time to time so that opportunities are not missed.

The distribution strategy is an important integral part of the brand proposition – develop it with care and forcefulness.

DESIRE? PROFITS?

A distribution channel's primary role is to make sure that those people who want a brand can actually get it, and get it in a better way than competitive products. In some cases, a particular distribution channel can provide an added dimension of relevance and appeal. Distribution costs can be significant – but they may well be worth it. A too narrow look at distribution can cause problems, a brand marketing perspective is needed to reach an optimal mix for all segments.

14
Step 7: the price to pay

In a perfect market, all identical items would carry the same price and if supply and/or demand changes, so would the price. That is the basic pricing principle first described by Adam Smith (1776) in *The Wealth of Nations*. The principle of market pricing is still valid but in its pure form rarely applies.

First, not all products are the same for everyone, one may prefer green another blue. The one preferring green will pay more for that than the blue one, and for the other individual, it is the other way around. A naive but real example, ask any car dealer with a showroom full of cars in the 'wrong' colour. There are also many other issues influencing the price. The timing – does the customer need it now or later so is there time to look for alternatives. The place – most consumers will pay more for a drink in a restaurant than in the supermarket, as illustrated previously. The features – a piece of furniture delivered and installed by the store will cost more than one that is flat-packed and taken home in a rented trailer.

Markets are not perfect. The people involved do not possess perfect information, they may not have access to many alternatives and above all the available alternatives are rarely identical. If the marketing departments have done their job properly, each product and service should be perceived as different from the others and thus not subjected to a direct comparison. While the principles of Adam Smith do apply, in reality each individual makes his or her own price value comparisons, and on the basis of the individual assessment makes a decision whether to buy or not.

Pricing is of course of fundamental importance to all companies. Price multiplied by volume generates the revenue that has to pay for salaries, raw materials, fixed overheads, etc. plus generate a profit. To get the price level right is difficult, most would agree. Too high a price, it will not sell. I once launched a range of frozen meals in the UK. Superb quality but too expensive. The range was closed down within 6 months. Too low a price, not enough profit. At the time of writing the world's coffee farmers are suffering from very low market prices on raw coffee beans. Not enough money to survive, let alone to save for the future.

In this chapter the different aspects of developing a price strategy for a customized brand are explored.

INDIVIDUALIZED MARKET PRICING

Many factors influence the price perception, as mentioned above. In each case a mini-market price process takes place each time a sale is made. The buyer concludes it is worth it, the seller that there is enough money in the price to be acceptable. Each time all the factors are metered into the considerations, and a decision is made.

The price level is also determined at the individual level by supply and demand, benefits and costs. Consequently, the price level will be different depending on location, time, distribution channel and service level, to mention a few factors. Different market segments will have different price expectations, and to understand these dynamics is of course crucial in maximizing the total revenue for a company.

A simple example: ice cream. The price of an ice cream cone sold by a street vendor is at one level, the same cone in a supermarket multi-pack will perhaps be some 20% lower and the same amount of ice cream sold in a tub is at a fraction of the cost of the cone. In addition, price elasticity changes. The street vendor has little to gain from selling at special low prices, while the supermarket may get a 100% uplift in sales if prices are reduced.

However, individual pricing is not practical in the majority of cases. For big industrial projects, of course, individual pricing is applied. For the consumer to buy a car there may be some individual flexibility in negotiating with the dealer. In most cases, the price is set according to the 'majority' position. The difference between mass-marketing and customized brand marketing is that the majority position in the first case is 'everyone', in the latter it is a segment or a particular occasion. How different depends on the perceived value by the particular customer at that time.

Pricing according to the perceived value by each segment is a practical way of managing pricing. For differentiated pricing to be credible, the different levels must be built around both the perceptions of the customers in question and the total market's view of pricing reality. In short, the different price levels must make sense to all. If not, those paying more will feel ripped off.

Structuring the pricing policy by segment can be difficult, but by distribution channel it is a viable option as per the Coca-Cola example in the previous chapter. Different prices in different channels make sense to people. In practice that is the most common way of pricing a customized brand. Taking each mini-segment of the market, consider that segment a marketplace in its own right with supply and demand and set the price accordingly.

For a more sophisticated pricing model the channel strategy can be overlaid with a pricing model for different features, adapting the pricing model to different requirements within a framework which makes sense to the customer universe.

Set the price by distribution channel to appeal to different segments.

PRICE TRANSPARENCY

Different prices in different places may seem like a strange concept, but in reality that is what is going on in most markets. Even if the list price is not differentiated, other price-related conditions such as service package and discounts certainly do differ making the actual price different from segment to segment.

Most customers understand that there are differences. After all, virtually all are exposed to sales from time to time when an item can be reduced by 50%. This is considered OK as there is an understandable and acceptable reason.

The guiding light is 'market pricing'. What is considered reasonable by the customers? The cost to make and deliver a product is not what should drive the pricing. Instead, the approach to take is, first, to set the price, then check whether it will make sufficient margin. If yes, go ahead of course. If not, consider if it can be made cheaper or if a higher price is feasible. Otherwise, don't sell, and focus on other products and services instead.

People accept that a specialist shop can be more expensive than a hypermarket. Furniture at IKEA is cheaper than on the High Street. The Coca-Cola example in the previous chapter is another example. These are credible differences because they make sense to the customer, the differentials reflect different levels of service and availability.

The same applies to business-to-business markets. A purchasing department is prepared to pay more for a product delivered with a substantial service package than one stripped of all types of support and guarantee. If something is customized to specific circumstances, the buyer is usually prepared to pay more. A new logo from a freelance graphic designer may cost £200, from a big reputable design agency the cost may well be £50,000 or more.

A pricing policy that will not succeed is one where the prices do not reflect the circumstances as the customer sees it. If a bank charges its existing customers more than new ones – the existing ones may well vote with their feet and change bank. Or, if the bank tries to charge for services which are perceived as cheap to run, customers will object, as they did when several UK banks tried to charge for using ATMs, making the ATM more expensive than over the counter service. Customers revolted and banks had to retreat.

The individual market price may also be based on different considerations than what the supplier has in mind. Loans offered over the telephone with fast processing carry in most countries a very high interest rate. While a traditional fully secured bank loan may be available for an 8% interest rate, an unsecured 'fast' loan costs over 20%. People still accept these 'fast' loans as the convenience is worth more than the inconvenience of going to the 'big bank', filling in all the papers and then having to wait for a decision.

In much the same way as a prepared food product costs much more than the ingredients, convenience is worth a price premium in certain situations.

Be honest and credible with pricing, different prices in different situations can make sense or create ill will. The former is better.

PRICING AND BRAND PERCEPTIONS

This is an area full of marketing myths. 'Low prices don't sell' in some markets. 'High prices don't sell' in other markets. The reality is that there is no one right answer but there are a few principles.

The first one is that it has to make sense, and make sense in the minds of the customers, not the suppliers. If a product is cheaper than others, people want to know why. If there is no answer, the assumption, at least from an unknown supplier, is that it is poor quality.

It works in a similar way if something is more expensive than the norm. With a few exceptions in the luxury markets, people will not buy something that is more expensive unless they are convinced there is a good reason. The reason may be rational or irrational. Rational reasons can be 'this is handmade by designer *XYZ*' or 'this is made from exquisite raw materials' when it comes to fashion or furniture, or more irrational ones can be 'there may be a future shortage so buy now and gain later', which was an argument for many to buy shares in Internet companies at an inflated high price in 2000.

Pricing also has to make sense for the supplier and companies in the distribution chain which is why a certain amount of discipline is required. The ice cream street vendor is not allowed or, perhaps more accurately, strongly discouraged by his supplier, to use other price points than those recommended by the supplier.

One reason is that brand perceptions would suffer due to consumer confusion if prices were hiked up on sunny days with high demand, and lowered on cloudy days with low demand. And confusion and strong brands do not go together, because a brand is supposed to represent trust and confidence – the opposite of confusion.

A way to avoid one element of confusion but potentially create another is to reconfigure products for different markets. For a loan to buy a house one set of interest rates and conditions apply, for a loan to buy a car it is another set. A jar of Nescafé in India is considerable cheaper than in the UK is another example. Both these make sense to most people although in both cases people try to exploit the situation. In the first case by borrowing money officially for the house but in reality to buy a car. In the second case by importing the product to the UK and make money on the difference.

A more sophisticated example, from the FMCG (fast-moving consumer goods) market, is that Nestlé Rowntree has been selling a special pack of After Eight mints to the German discount retailer Aldi so that Aldi can sell at a low price and other German retailers, charging a higher price, will avoid direct price comparisons.

These examples are all acceptable to the customers as long as they are sensible. A product is expected to be cheaper in Aldi so the differences probably do not cause any problems.

The price of a product, though, is a very tangible aspect of the brand. It is easy to compare, and is a favourite subject of politicians and other officials as it is easy to explain and argue about. From a brand perspective it requires great sensitivity and consistency. If a brand is priced at a certain level, for whatever reasons, it makes sense to maintain that price level in relation to other brands even if that may mean £10 in one channel and £25 in another.

Be prepared to explain price differentials and don't create confusion.

DESIRE? PROFITS?

The price of a product is the final determinator of whether a purchase will take place or not. In that way it has great influence. Price levels can also build relevance in that customers may feel that, at a certain price, the product is good value for money. The variable needs to be managed with the greatest care as the wrong price can lose a lot of business.

Pricing is key to profit. Adjusting price levels has been known to boost net earnings by 5 percentage points or even more. But, profit is price multiplied by volume, so the balance has to be right and each segment reviewed for optimal results – within the overall framework.

15

Step 8: from 'interesting' to 'just right for me'

In the 21st century, most marketing executives' ultimate dream is still to be responsible for making a commercial for mainstream television. In reality very few of them will get the opportunity as the majority of brands do not feature on television, and for those that do making a commercial is in most cases a project handled high up in the organization by a select few. But marketing communications is much more than television, magazine and outdoor advertising. It is direct marketing, interactive marketing, PR, word-of-mouth, events and much more.

Most marketing communication is mass-market-oriented, created in most cases with a specific target audience in mind but structured so that it will appeal to a wide audience. The exception is direct private media such as direct mail, but in most cases this highly personal media is still treated as mass media as well – the same message to all. Very often the same credit card offer is sent to everyone who falls into a certain category without any consideration of the individual's circumstances.

To build a customized brand requires a different outlook, an outlook based on segmentation and individual attention. Though, the similarity is that, as with any communication, unless the brief is clear and to the point, it takes a genius to create good communication. And geniuses are few and far between and most of them are very expensive. With a good brief, however, 'all' it takes is good craftsmanship to deliver excellent results. And I mean no disrespect to craftsmen or women. Many marketing professionals, including the author, have the highest regard for craftsmen and prefer to work with them rather than creative teams who pretend they are geniuses (and most of them aren't).

The purpose of the chapter is to look at some of the key elements of marketing communication in a world of customized brands. It does not in any respect cover all aspects but I hope covers enough to inspire marketers to apply the right mix of strategic skill, analytical conclusions and creative flair to move a brand from being 'interesting' to 'that's what I really want'.

GET THE BRIEF AND STRATEGY RIGHT

In the same way as with product development and other marketing activities the brief is much more important with a customized approach. The reason is that as it is expected to result in the development of a number of different adaptations, discipline is required to ensure that all stays on track. To do that a distinct brief is essential.

The brief does not only have to be 'right', in a customised branding environment it can, and should, contain much more information – or direction on how to get additional information – as well. All the information from the segmentation process must be included, along with the data to be interpreted from the perspective of communication and, of course, the adapted brand platform by segment. From this strategic raw material, it is possible to develop a main communication platform.

The next step is to take the main platform and adapt it to each segment from a communication point of view. This is one area where the multidimensional segmentation approach described earlier can be very effective. To develop an attractive style for the communication, life stage segmentation can be a very useful first step. The creative style to attract an 18-year-old is different from that required for a 65-year-old. For one thing, in the latter case the typeface has to be bigger than in the former. The 18-year-old may well feel more insecure and require a more traditional approach than the 65-year-old 'who has been there, done that' and may prefer something a bit more light-hearted.

Regarding the creative content, however, life stage may not be the best segmentation model. It may well be that a lifestyle approach will work better, or perhaps even a straightforward gender, income and education level-based segmentation.

The development of the message mix has to take into consideration the requirements of not only each segment but also the totality. As described previously, in developing a customized brand proposition the totality must make sense, what is said to each segment must fit together and build a unit like a family of children with their individual characteristics but yet a strong sense of coming from the same place. The message and media cannot be developed for one segment at a time but for the brand as a totality first, and each segment to follow.

A message for one group must not alienate others or even worse contradict what is said to another group. All messages must fit together and work as an orchestra. Different instruments and sounds but working together in harmony for a great result.

From this it follows that the marketing communication programme becomes more complex. This in turn means that it is crucial that (a) the brief and strategy is documented from the beginning and any changes are also documented and (b) all efforts are made to simplify matters. The first point is to ensure the process stays on track. The second point is to avoid overcomplicating things unnecessarily. A complex way of working in a complex environment is just too much complexity and will, in most cases, end up in disaster.

Document the brief and the strategy to keep the process on track.

GET THE TARGETING AND MESSAGE RIGHT

Segmented marketing communication is of course nothing new. Any reasonably sized media plan has an element of segmentation to it. But in the overwhelming majority of cases, segmentation is applied to media selection, not the message. There are some obvious examples of message segmentation, such as Nescafé UK running a special youth campaign targeting young, potential coffee drinkers portraying the drink as an alternative to soft drinks while the main campaign is more traditional. But these are exceptions. Most campaigns use one message and then segment the media buying to get best possible cost-effectiveness.

More sophisticated targeting takes place in other market sectors. Financial services is one such sector. Financial services and in particular those with a considerable amount of information per customer has in some isolated instances achieved considerable success – while, perhaps not surprisingly, others remain in a mass-market mode even today.

One European bank had already started this process 15 years ago by collecting customer information in a structured way. They now have for each customer around 1,000 different criteria to classify each particular individual. A criteria group can include how often the individual draws money from the ATM and frequency of use of his or her payment card in shops; another criteria group may cover the ownership of different savings products.

On the basis of this information the customer database is divided into 15–20 segments, and within each segment further selection is made depending on the product offer. For each campaign, the most appropriate segments, usually 1–3, are selected and from those specific clusters are identified where, based on experience and assumptions, the response is likely to be excellent.

The strict targeting has two effects. First, waste is avoided: rather than mailing millions, thousands are sent the offers. The advantage of this is not only a saving by the bank but it also avoids annoying customers who are not interested. Second, the response rates reach levels previously unheard of in financial services. Between 70% and 80% of targeted customers giving a positive response is not unusual. And, it can be 'serious money'. On the basis of one mailing in 20+ variants to selected subgroups, over £20 million were transferred from one type of savings to another. At the time, a significant achievement.

It is worth noting in these particular cases that the creative executions were basically a letter, well-crafted but not constituting groundbreaking creativity. The success was totally due to extremely well-identified targets and total customer understanding leading to the bank being able to feature the most appropriate arguments in the letters to the customers in a language relevant to the recipient. This is an example of a creative team using customer data to be able to produce totally relevant communication.

We once developed segmented brand propositions for a brand of coffee. The target audience was split into four different segments based on behaviour.

Segment 1 consisted of loyal users. The strategy was to 'keep them happy'. They had chosen this brand, they were happy with it and the communication strategy was based on reassurance: 'You have made the right choice'. The communication enforced basic coffee values, such as superior raw materials, 'best beans', carefully processed and packed. Admittedly not very exciting or earth-shattering communication but that was not necessary as these customers were already converted. However, what was important was to ensure they would continue to buy the brand and could explain to their friends and family members why they should continue to buy the brand.

Segment 2 was made up of heavy users of coffee who only bought the brand intermittently. Coffee is a very competitive market and the promiscuous consumer (buying different brands within a repertoire – the most common behaviour in the majority of consumer goods markets) has much to choose from. The message was much stronger than Segment 1. It was about lifestyle and pushed forward one key element of the brand – that it was colourful and full of life. All the elements needed to provide impact even if it meant losing some of the more subtle messages.

Segment 3 consumers were the occasional users of coffee and of the brand. The theme was built around the pleasures of having a cup of coffee, turning a boring day into something a bit more colourful, pleasant and relaxing.

Segment 4 included those who only were drinking coffee on special occasions. Commercially this is not an important segment but a proposition was still developed. It was based around a communication strategy focused on 'if you do drink coffee, make sure you choose the best.'

In reality the brand was not very big, it was 'half-way' into a launch phase and resources were limited. To achieve effective marketing communication Segments 1 and 2 were chosen as the focus of activity while Segments 3 and 4 were basically neglected.

The actual marketing communication was segmented in both the media and the message. Segment 1, the loyal users, a small group as the brand was fairly new, were given their message via the label and on-pack material. This was informative with the copy based around the thought that these people were knowledgeable about coffee (must be to choose such a good coffee), understood how to make a good cup of coffee, would be interested in more information about where the coffee came from, where it was grown, etc., all the time assuming that this was not completely new to the consumer but more in the spirit of 'I am sure you know but you may not know the full story so we will tell you a bit more . . .'.

The Segment 2 communication strategy was also the 'public' strategy. These consumers were the ones who needed to be properly converted, become less promiscuous and more loyal to the brand. The creative strategy was developed into a television commercial and a segmented mass-market media strategy was used to reach this target group.

As illustrated by this example, the process to develop a customized brand proposition, when the building blocks and information is in place, does not have to be complicated. It is not necessary to have 10–15 segments to achieve a higher degree of effectiveness than the traditional form of mass-market advertising. A strategy based on 3–4 segments will be a great improvement compared with no segmentation at all.

The first step in developing communication, once the objectives have been defined, is to ensure that the segmentation and thus the targeting is right. The segmentation must be appropriate to be able (a) to develop relevant communication from a content point of view and (b) to be able to plan a programme of getting the message to the audience. The second part of this is to get the right message to the right audience. The starting point is the brand message and from that base variants are developed to suit each subcategory.

Distinct targeting and message can generate amazing results.

FROM MONOLOGUE TO DIALOGUE

The 'Holy Grail' for many marketing executives is to achieve customer dialogue, going from the traditional brand mono-logue – telling the audience – to brand dialogue – telling and getting a response back, building a dialogue.

Although far from all customers want to get into a dialogue with a supplier, almost all want to have the opportunity. So, as most companies have discovered, there must be a way to contact the supplier. With all digital media and telephone systems this is in theory easy and something most FMCG (fast-moving consumer goods) companies have provided for the last 20–30 years. Banks and other professional suppliers have followed suit, and today most financial and other institutions have a channel for customers to get in touch. Many other industries fail.

Try writing a personal note to AOL, arguable the world's best-known email service provider in the year 2002. There will be no response beyond an automatic acknowledgement. Try to get beyond the AOL helpline to talk to a person in management position – not possible. The result, poor brand values and customer retention only because it is too difficult to change supplier. Not a way to build a customized brand while in theory all Internet-based companies have glowing opportunities due to the richness of customer data profiles.

For brand credibility it is crucial that the channels from the customers actually work.

> The Virgin group, run by Sir Richard Branson, makes great play of the accessibility of Sir Richard. For instance, as a passenger on a Virgin Atlantic aircraft the passenger is encouraged to write to him. However, for brand credibility it is essential that the letters get answered. (No, I am afraid Sir Richard and his staff chose to ignore two letters I wrote to him.)

The next step, after opening up a functioning communication channel, which by now most companies have, is to build a dialogue with those customers who would like to have an active contact. Internet chat rooms, proper telephone advice (not only receiving comments but quality response) and traditional letter writing are all useful techniques.

> It has been claimed that, of British Airways' over 40,000 gold card users, the vast majority believe that they have a personal dialogue with the person in charge of the card scheme in the company. This from a group, presumably mainly experienced business travellers, that should be able to realize that this is not practically possible and that the letters must be tailored in an automatic way. A victory for style and content.

The rules of engagement are simple. Open a channel, encourage dialogue, respond in a positive and interesting way and, if possible, give those opening up a dialogue a good reason to continue to do so. And the reason should be 'content', not sales promotion activity. People contacting a company do so in most cases for a specific reason, and if the contact is proving fruitful, the individuals will continue to get in touch and stay supportive of the brand.

The exception is when the purpose is to increase awareness

and top of mind. An entertaining website, or telephone numbers with great humour content, can be ways of getting into a dialogue with specific categories. In such a case the creative strategy is more in the field of advertising than dialogue as the dialogue will only continue for as long as the entertainment value is there. It can be a perfectly viable strategy, used by companies such as Coca-Cola and the Tango orange drink, but strategically it is not dialogue but entertaining advertising.

Open the communication channels but only promise a dialogue if you can deliver.

ENGAGING THE CUSTOMERS – AND OTHERS – WITH PASSION

Targeting is one way of using data and information in a quantitative way to achieve highly effective communication. A totally different way of achieving customer engagement is to use flair and personal initiative. Even though to customize the brand is best done on the basis of data-driven brand marketing, it is not the only way. Fortunately there are other ways of getting into a customer dialogue and get many people involved.

Harley-Davidson (H-D) is one brand where customer relationships nowadays take centre stage. It was not always so. Originally a traditional US motorbike, the brand was close to being hijacked by Hell's Angels and the like. A distinct profile for sure but the number of Hell's Angels is fairly limited, so not much potential. Instead, H-D took charge of the brand by channelling and developing customer engagement to such an extent that it was almost 'built into' the brand.

H-D has a 640,000-member owners' club as a key vehicle to its customers. The owners' club organizes events, brings people together and communicates with them. Through the owners' club you get access to a 720-page catalogue of parts and accessories, where you not only buy traditional spare parts but also blue jeans and pickup trucks.

Passion, even of the H-D kind, does not manage itself. Half the company employees own an H-D. To own and ride is the only true way of experiencing the brand. H-D almost lost control of the brand in the 1970s to the Hell's Angels. Now H-D are facing another threat. The average age of a Harley buyer is 46, up from 37 in 1990. The problem is not that the target audience will disappear into the graveyard, but who wants to buy a bike that is driven by old people? Not the old people who buy Harleys – they ride a bike to feel young. Consequently H-D is segmenting the product range by launching 'younger profile' bike models to balance the age pyramid.

Finally, the company is successful, selling every bike it makes, with growing sales and profits.

H-D has many of the hallmarks of a traditional 'emotional' brand. It is a luxury item, many famous people drive one, it has featured in movies and its usage is related to pure pleasure – going for a ride at the weekend or on holiday. All this makes it easier to generate passion, but it is not a necessity to be able to build an emotional bond as 'there is no such thing as a boring product – only boring marketing'.

Eddie Stobart Ltd is a UK haulage company, running trucks across the UK and the rest of Europe. Trucking in some parts of the world, such as the USA, has a certain glamour. There is a whole category in country music devoted to trucking. Not so in the UK. Trucking is distinctly unglamorous and is held in high regard by very, very few. In such a market Eddie Stobart has carved a unique niche.

Eddie Stobart is probably the only truck company with a fan club. It has a devoted following of people who have formed a fan club with over 25,000 members. As a member you get access to where the trucks run, so that you can 'spot different trucks' for your collection of truck numbers, members can buy merchandise and participate in various activities.

> Why does Eddie Stobart trucks have such a following? There are probably many reasons. The two main ones are that the truck drivers are neat and tidy (enough to get a distinct profile in the UK in this industry) and that Eddie Stobart himself obviously has a talent for engaging not only customers but many others as well.
>
> For the company there is a great, additional benefit. Profits from merchandise help the P&L (profit and loss) account considerably, especially in years when the trucking business is suffering from overcapacity, low prices and intense competition.

If a marketing department gets access to a lot of customer data it is easy to get totally involved in the quantitative side of marketing analysis and strategy. It is important to remember that one should 'always' aim to get the best of both worlds, systematic analysis and creative inspiration.

Passion has a great place in marketing.

LEAVE THE MEDIA TARGETING TO THE TARGET GROUP

This heading is perhaps somewhat provocative in the context of this book, but in the marketing mix there are some media which to a large extent rely on the target group to do the selection. This is a parallel to the self-selection product customization described in Chapter 12. Self-selecting media are in total contrast to highly targeted ones such as direct mail. Marketing techniques that fall into this category of *laissez-faire* are activities such as Public Relations (PR) and word-of-mouth marketing.

In any media there is an element of self-selection. Targeted magazine or television advertising reaches many outside the intended target audience. Even a direct mail piece may not be opened by the person it was intended for but someone else who is not in the defined target group. A recipient of the communication can take in the message, or choose to ignore it.

With media that rely on others to do the main part of the communication, like PR and word-of-mouth, self-selection is a fairly reliable tool. People who are not interested will just not bother. If a person is not interested in sports, he or she will just ignore the sports reports. Brand messages are no different. If BMW is of no interest but Mercedes-Benz is, the individual will pick up a message about Mercedes but not BMW. If family features of a car are of interest, that information will be read or talked about; if not, the messages will just flow by.

One fascinating aspect, and a challenging one, is that especially with word-of-mouth you never know how it is going to work out. The Eddie Stobart example above is mainly the result of word-of-mouth, the early success of Hard Rock Café was totally an effect of word-of-mouth and likewise many cult status brands have their origins in more or less managed word-of-mouth campaigns.

One example of combining word-of-mouth with confident sales techniques is the 'energy' drink Red Bull in the UK. When the brand was originally launched, the budget for the launch was very limited, £50,000 according to the management at the time. Such a budget does not buy much of anything so the only option available was to adopt a guerrilla marketing approach that is as old as marketing, but in the right environment will still work.

The strategic decision was made to launch in London and that the trendy bars/pubs were the place where the product should be seen. If available in those outlets, the theory was, the rest would in due course follow. A strategy that in retrospect we can see was successful.

The approach was to assign different bars to different people. Then these individuals would go from bar to bar and ask for Red Bull. If the answer was no, they were told to just say thank you and leave. After having repeated the sequence a couple of times, a salesperson would call the bar for a regular sales call. And, more likely than not, an order would be forthcoming. When on display in the bar, the next phase was to come back and ask for Red Bull again. This time the individual would drink it with great

> pleasure thus showing there is a demand and that it is a great drink.

The particular creative style and communication approach of Red Bull makes it self-selecting. People who approve of such an irreverent approach will go for it, others will ignore it. Self-selection at work.

Self-selecting targeting can at times be the best way.

INDIVIDUALIZE WHEREVER POSSIBLE

For proponents and students of one-to-one marketing this is 'old stuff', which indeed it is. So, we include it more to ensure a reasonably complete picture. The more appropriate a piece of communication is, the better. The more uniquely it has been tailored to the specific needs of the individual, the better. This tailoring of the message involves adapting the message and, where appropriate, using the name of the respondent.

Developments in technology have opened up a great number of new ways to communicate, such as viral marketing (creating video clips of such high entertainment value that they get sent around the world) and SMS messaging.

> An example of different media use by the Boston Symphony Orchestra was reported in the Peppers & Rogers newsletter. The objective was to get as many as possible of 35,000 'lapsed' patrons, who had not responded to any activity over the last two years, to return to the Orchestra. The individuals were encouraged to log on to a special website using a unique registration code. On connecting the 'ex-patron' was greeted with a customized audio and video message, starting with a personalized greeting and then followed by an appropriate music clip and a special offer for concert tickets.

> The response rate was 10% with a conversion rate of around 3%, which given that these were lapsed customers must be considered a good result.

Using the name of the target is an 'old trick' in direct marketing – which does not make it less effective. The original reason is to clearly show who the message is intended for. In today's world it is also a sign of professionalism, especially in business-to-business. If the potential supplier has not taken the trouble to write the name of the customer on a mailing or message, the supplier gives the impression of not being professional – 'if they can't write direct mail correctly, can they actually deliver a product or service?'

However, an even greater mistake is to get the name wrong. I personally receive many mailings to Mr Wilson, not Mr Nilson. Hardly a way to build brand values, more a way to destroy brand values. Another mistake is to send material to people who no longer work at a company – 10 years after leaving the Nestlé Company in the UK, a UK direct mail magazine (yes, it is true) sent a magazine in my name to my previous employer.

Individualize as much as possible, but get it right.

MASS-MEDIA FOR TARGETING OR TARGETED MEDIA FOR MASS-MARKETING?

Choosing media for a communication campaign should in most cases be an objective exercise in evaluating the most cost-effective method to reach the audience and then make any necessary adaptation due to creative content and style. But, many media decisions are based on subjective assessments of media channels.

True mass-marketing in the literal sense is, as has been argued elsewhere in the book, not a very effective approach in most cases. Though, real mass-marketing, reaching the mass market in whatever way appropriate, is still of great importance, and to customize your brand is the best way of achieving this. Consequently, the most targeted of media, such as direct mail, can be effective in reaching the mass-market if structured the right way.

> The *IKEA Catalogue*, the world's biggest publication, is distributed in most IKEA markets door-to-door. Direct mail by any other name, sometimes addressed, sometimes not but always with a distribution plan that is based on decisions regarding who to reach – which in the case of IKEA is, more often than not, every household in a region.

To do the reverse, using mass-media for targeted activities can be an interesting challenge. In many market sectors, television advertising is the most effective media. It is in colour, has moving pictures with sound and it is possible to tell a story. It is even possible to add an interactive link. However, traditionally it is seen as a media with high entrance costs.

> In a project with Carlton television, the ITV station for the London region covering an area with some 10 million people, our company developed a strategy to reach a segment of the market using mainstream television – for a new Colombian instant coffee brand called Buendia. By carefully selecting a stratum of the Carlton viewing audience and utilizing the programming profile, it was possible with a limited budget of less than £100,000 to reach 34% of all ABC1 housewives (according to the UK classification) in the greater London area, in total around 1 million, with a frequency of 3+. In addition, the other block to using television advertising, the cost of making a commercial, was overcome by a unique co-operation with Carlton studios making it possible to produce a commercial for a fraction of the 'normal' cost (approx. £25,000 compared to £150,000). The result? Sales increased by 50% in the supermarkets and a fourfold increase in awareness.

Building a segmented media plan as in the case of Buendia is an integral part of developing marketing communications for a customized brand. For optimal results it is prudent to review all media channels to ensure best cost-effectiveness. The cheapest media can sometimes be the most effective.

When flying British Airways to Florida with my family, we had, of course, economy class tickets. No frills is the way to go with a big family. When seated on the plane the stewardess approach me and asked whether everything was OK, did I want a special newspaper or refreshments and leaving with 'do let me know if I can help you'. Why did she do this? Not because of my blue eyes and grey hair but because I had a BA Gold card as a frequent flyer. The marginal cost to British Airways for this communication was almost nil. The effect on me was that my appreciation of BA went up considerably and my family was most impressed. The cost-effectiveness was very high and 'all' it took was a piece of co-ordination between the BA database and the passenger lists.

Another example of using mass-media to influence key decision-makers is an activity carried out by a former colleague of mine. His task, which was difficult, was to convince the buyer of a retail chain to list the new range of products he was introducing. One hurdle to pass was to convince the buyer that this new brand actually was a 'big advertised brand'. The way to do it was to track the route where the buyer was driving to work. Then poster sites along this route were bought and plastered with posters advertising the brand. Very targeted communication to reach a target group of one, using a mass-media seen by thousands.

In many ways different marketing communication channels are compartmentalized. Sending things through the post is direct marketing and terrestrial television advertising is mass-marketing. An objective view of what is needed and a creative look at available media may come up with interesting and unusual media recommendations.

Don't let convention rule the media mix.

THE INVERTED MEDIA MIX

The process of properly building a customized brand leads to a change in how to deal with the media mix. Moving the focus from the mass to the segment and individual changes the perspective.

The traditional approach, especially in consumer markets but increasingly in business-to-business as well, is that display advertising in the form of television, newspapers, magazines, billboards, etc. is considered the most important part of the media mix, the one forming the base for the whole creative strategy. This form of advertising is seen as the main vehicle for developing the communication platform and to get the brand proposition across even though other parts of the communication mix may have a higher spend and effectiveness.

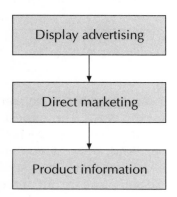

The second category, direct marketing, is mostly used in a tactical sense, driving direct response to specific offers made within the brand framework. It is rarely given the role of building the brand, more to exploit the brand's perceptions for short-term gains.

The third element in this simplified model is product information. This is the kind of information, on paper or digitally, that is usually handed over at the point of purchase to help the user to make full use of the product. Typical examples are instruction manuals or conditions for use of a credit card. The production and design of the former are often handed over to the most junior people, or staff with little involvement in the marketing activities of the company. The latter appears to be done by legal departments. They are produced with functionality and low costs in mind and, as a result, almost never fulfil a brand-building role, more often it is a brand-devaluing role as the instructions are difficult to follow and conditions of use difficult to understand.

If a customized branding approach is applied, and some additional common sense, the media mix will be turned around, inverted.

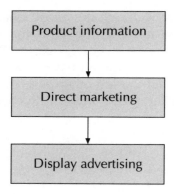

The individual is the most important person, and how do you reach him or her the best way? The easiest way is to use the communication channel that has been opened by the delivery of the product (or service). And, how do you ensure that there is a repeat purchase in due course? By making sure that the buyer gets the greatest possible use and pleasure out of the product or service.

There are two good reasons for starting the communication process at the heart of the brand, the product or service. The information that accompanies the product will first enhance the product experience, making usage of the product a greater pleasure than otherwise. Second, it will also communicate and 'live' the brand values, the brand proposition and glow of brand personality.

And, in most instances it is cheap. Targeting is 100%, no waste at all, and distribution is virtually for free. Production cost is the only expense, but as the unit needs to be produced anyway the low oncost makes it in most cases a very cost-effective medium.

The second step in the communications flow is still direct marketing but the role changes. There is of course nothing wrong with driving results, after all if the short term is not taken care of, there will not be a long term. But it is a wasted opportunity to focus on short-term results only. With proper understanding of the audience, with distinct targeting as to who gets what and with an individualized approach, it can be an effective tool for building the brand. The *IKEA Catalogue* is not only distributed to get people to the store, it is there to build the IKEA brand. *Reader's Digest*, the 'old master' of direct marketing, gets brand values across alongside distinct offers. But most brands fail – ignoring opportunities to communicate with the target audience.

Third, display advertising. Is it necessary? From the above one can get the impression that it is not. Far from it, and for three different reasons.

The first one is that display advertising, almost regardless of media, can still be a cost-effective way of reaching many at a low unit cost. Because of the structure of the media, cost per individual contact is low, and for a brand reaching many it is cost-effective. This applies not only to consumer goods but also to many business-to-business brands. Display advertising in trade journals is often an inexpensive option. As long as the message appeals to a relatively large proportion of the audience, it is worth considering for this reason alone.

The second reason is that display advertising is a good way of fishing for customers outside known waters, growing the customer base. New customers within existing segments may be found through other media, but, as most customer universes evolve in a dynamic way, to be totally silent to a wider potential audience may not be a good idea. The spillover of display advertising can build up opportunities for finding new customers, or indeed individuals who are about to enter the market.

These two reasons are generally acknowledged and taken into account. The third reason is very important but often ignored and it is that a successful brand needs to be seen as 'socially acceptable'. Display advertising, because it is a public medium, has the effect of making something be seen as 'generally known', to be a product, to quote the advertising legend David Ogilvy's father, 'well spoken of in the advertisements'. Direct marketing and product information are private media that can be highly effective with the individual, but that is all.

There is a considerable comfort factor in owning a product that is widely advertised, at least if the advertising is making the product desirable. The majority of new car advertising is aimed at giving reassurance to those who have already bought the car. The role is to make sure that the new owner will feel pleased with the purchase and in due course buy the brand again, and that the owner's friends and family will think the decision was well made and not criticize the purchase.

This effect is of fundamental importance in business-to-business advertising as well. All executives involved in a purchase like to feel that they have done the right thing. Having bought something known from display media provides a comfort factor of considerable importance.

Get the best out of each part of the inverted media mix.

FOCUS

With segmented marketing communications most executives have to make a choice. Which segment to prioritize? With a complex marketing mix, the risks are high that it all becomes very little to very many subgroups with very little total effect due to fragmentation. Focus to achieve enough impact is crucial. To what extent the communication to one segment has to be sacrificed to reach effectiveness in another has to be dealt with on a case by case basis, but whatever the approach, focus is essential.

Focus means less is more.

DESIRE? PROFITS?

First a warning. The brand experience has to deliver on the promise. The whole dotcom balloon collapsed because of lack of delivery of the promise. Marketing communication is the tool to move from an 'oh, yeah' product to 'yes, I want it'. By making the message more relevant and by using media channels that are close to the individual in combination with general activities to build acceptance, the brand can move from acceptance to exceptional desire. Nike and BMW were not accidents, they were the results of great products and focused communication.

Marketing communication can be the greatest waster of money, if done badly, or the best revenue earner there is, if done right. Every activity needs to be costed and followed up to ensure that the communication to each segment is cost-effective in the short and/or long term.

16

Step 9: make it move – sales promotion in a customized world

Sales promotion was one of the first marketing activities to apply some of the thinking behind customizing the brand; namely, by targeting the promotion and making it relevant to the recipient would increase chances for a positive response.

There is an important distinction between traditional, targeted, sales promotion techniques and using sales promotion in the customized branding sense. The difference was explained indirectly in the section on the inverted marketing communication mix in Chapter 15 (p. 139). The difference is essentially that traditional sales promotion has only one objective – get sales – while sales promotion for a customized brand has an additional objective, which is to build the brand. From this it follows that strategy, content, execution and targeting need to be designed so that they actually build the brand within the target segment and not, as many promotions do, exploit the brand values for short-term gain.

The purpose of this chapter is not to cover the subject in any detail as much has been written already on the subject, but more to highlight a few aspects of particular importance and relevance in the context of building a brand.

THE GOOD NEWS

Any direct marketing person 'worth his salt' will be able to verify that targeted segment promotions are more effective than those that have a mass-market design. It is also so in the vast majority of cases that the oncost for segmenting and targeting is significantly less than the improvement in effectiveness.

It has also been proven in several studies that sales promotion activities, especially price-driven promotions, are much more effective when driving new brands and products into the market-place, growing the penetration, than they are when used on their own for trying to bring new life to old products. In the former case the money is usually well spent, in the latter the extra activity may even accelerate the decline.

> A typical example of short-term activity is fund-raising for charities. We planned and executed a programme to raise money for a UK hospice which resulted in an over sevenfold return on marketing investment despite the fact that the target group area, restricted geographically, was limited. The key to success was simply selected targeting and striking creative execution based on a well-considered brand strategy.

Sales promotions have a great advantage in that the short-term effects can easily be measured. Though, this must not become a trap for the brand builder. Effective sales promotion activities have short- *and* long-term effects.

Sales promotion is, though, the area within the customized brand marketing mix where the short-term effects are likely to be greatest. To offer a new product or introduce a new distribution channel strategy takes more time, usually involves much more activity and takes longer to get results. With sales promotion, the results come quickly in the majority of cases.

> The Tesco Clubcard's initial success was based on the programme's success as a sales promotion tool. At the time of the launch of the programme, Tesco immediately gained market share points. This was due to many factors. It was a new initiative, it was very well introduced, the offers were

interesting, etc. The Clubcard is an interesting example of the mix between short and long term. The scheme would most probably not have survived if the initial sales promotion effect had not taken place. It is equally fair to assume that the Clubcard would not have survived in the longer term without the strategic use of the customer data generated by the programme.

For a company or brand starting with a customization strategy, the sales promotion part is not to be ignored. Short-term effects, early wins, are important for a strategy to gain acceptance internally and with shareholders. As the long-term effects by definition take time to materialize and that it also takes time to generate enough customer data to develop a successful brand strategy (if this is not already available), the short-term results can make or break the strategy.

It works. Use it to start building a customized brand.

THE BAD NEWS

The biggest problem with sales promotion ideas is that they are often easy to imitate. An offer by one brand can easily be replicated by another, neutralizing any gains. This is always a problem with sales promotions regardless of the brand strategy, but tying the activity to a distinct brand strategy does 'help' in that the activity is not only about sales promotion but also building the brand. However, there is no way around the imitation problem, the only advisable route is to learn and improve continuously to stay ahead of competition.

Another problem is that it is not that difficult to get it wrong, especially when it comes to promotions through direct marketing. As mentioned previously it is essential when using targeted media to get everything right, correct name, correct address, correct reference to products already bought.

Barclaycard runs an extensive direct marketing programme for its credit card in the UK. Like most companies they have a range of different types of card. To increase the penetration of Barclaycard Gold a promotion was planned and executed – the proposition was fairly standard with offers of no fee, insurance, purchase cover, etc. and with the mailing came an application form. Could have been a good promotion if it had not been addressed to a holder of Barclaycard Platinum (next tier up card). By sending this mailing to a person definitely outside the largest group, the effect of the promotion was of course zero. However, the effect on the brand perception was negative because making mistakes with mailing lists did not inspire confidence in Barclaycard being able to 'take good care of my money'. Would anyone feel comfortable trusting their money with a company who can't even get a mailing list right?

And, perhaps not surprisingly, the mailing did not contain any significant brand building message.

Finally, whether bad news or not it is worth noting that sales promotions may not be necessary nor a good thing. It is unusual to see sales promotion activities for consultancy services or investment products for heavy industry. The reason is of course that these types of product and service do not respond to a short-term promotion as the decision-making process is, as a rule, lengthy so a promotional activity will not generate any immediate return.

Be quick to avoid imitation. Get it right. Don't do it unless it will build the brand.

DESIRE? PROFITS?

The role of sales promotion is to convert someone who is considering buying to actually make the decision. It will not make the brand conceptually more desirable, but a few 'extras' may well be what turns a prospective into a converted customer.

Sales promotions need to be tracked and measured to ensure the money is well spent. Spending money on rising stars may well prove to be a good investment; to try to use promotion to bring life to a tired brand is not a sensible strategy.

17

Step 10: clinching the deal

Personal selling is as old as business, it has been around for thousands of years. Personal selling is also the most appropriate tool for customized branding. The whole process can be customized to each customer's requirements and, if the salesperson is skilled, be adapted even during the sales process to changing requirements. It is perhaps ironic that the part of the marketing mix with the longest tradition, personal selling, is the one that is most targeted, while the latest addition (email) is in the vast majority of cases the least targeted with millions of people getting the same message in the hope that someone somewhere will respond.

In this chapter, some key elements of the sales approach will be considered from the perspective of customizing the brand.

THE COST–BENEFIT DILEMMA

The power of personal sales calls can be considerable, and many customers like to deal with a human being. It is possible to buy new cars on the Internet, but few do. One reason is the lack of personal attention. But the cost of the sales call must be justified in the minds of the customers. When it comes to groceries and many other consumer goods, the consumers have decided that personal service is really not all that important, hence the disappearance of the small shop with personal service and the growth of big self-service units. The extra cost for personal service is not worth the benefit.

The role of the personal sales process will of course, in particular due to this cost–benefit situation, differ from market sector to market sector. A big industrial investment is hardly made by direct mail, but by personal sales calls followed up by proposals and quotes, mostly delivered in person. A consultancy proposal can be modified and changed during a sales call so that the final proposal is as relevant and appealing as possible. On the other hand, to buy a car insurance policy, a simple telephone call to a call centre is for most the perfect personal service. The combination of personal service and low costs was the reason for the rise and considerable initial success of Direct Line, a telephone-based insurance company in the UK.

Great effect – but will it pay?

MAKING IT EFFECTIVE

The personal sales process has two advantages. One, it is a way of collecting information about the customer. Two, it is an effective way of persuading and tailoring a message and product to a customer's requirements.

Many salesforces still use the salesforce for both functions. Others have found more efficient, and better, ways of collecting information so that the salesperson can focus on what is really required, customizing the proposal at the point of sale.

> The Brazilian AmBev Brewery has a 12,000 strong salesforce calling on outlets across the country. Each salesperson has a digital 'assistant' with up-to-date information on each of the million places where the brewery sells its products. In that way the salesperson has full access to information, can adapt pricing and promotional offers depending on sales and share of trade in each outlet, customizing the offer in each individual case.

When the UK utilities market (water, sewage, electricity, gas, etc.) was deregulated, it set off a 'wild scramble' to take customers from competitors. Each household was inundated with offers of cheaper electricity from the gas supplier, cheaper gas from the electricity supplier and even cheaper offers if the customer bought all from the same supplier. In the end relatively few changed supplier, several who did were disappointed as the most attractive offers sometimes turned out to be presented by companies that had difficulty getting connections and billing the customers correctly. One of the more well-established and 'serious' companies soon realized that just mailing households would not generate any brand switch, apart from those who would switch all the time taking advantage of various promotional offers.

The utilities company in question concluded, first, that in order to achieve a proper switch of loyalties, a personal call was required. The second conclusion was that to let sales-people walk the streets and cold-call was not a very efficient way of operating. The initial response to this was to estimate where the most likely prospects for change live and then call on these households. This also proved to be not very effective.

A much more successful approach was based on customer insight and segmentation. The first action was to map those who had already switched to try and find out why they switched and to understand who these customers were. Where did they live, what kind of household, what kind of dwelling, income level, etc. The second action was, on the basis of this information, to mail and then follow up by a personal call the most likely prospects for changing. By developing and refining a model for this the conversion rates on sales calls increased by over 1,000%.

To be able to customize a brand proposition at the point of sale, the salesperson must have a full grasp of all variables available. This does require a better trained and informed salesperson than one who is just out to sell one product in one format. For a more sophisticated sales situation, a perceptive ability to understand the customer, and what would be relevant to the customer, can be crucial. This in turn puts demands on marketing management, first, to trust the salesperson to take decisions on the spot and, second, to provide enough information to make an efficient sales call a possibility.

Much more can be said about sales and sales management in this context. It is a specialist subject and for more information several books and websites are available.

Don't ask salespeople to provide marketing with information – they want to sell. Give them the best possible information for efficient sales calls.

DESIRE? PROFITS?

The personal sales call can be an ideal place to add the extra dimension to a product or service that will make it highly desirable. Provide the salesperson with information beforehand so that the initial offer is totally relevant and the sales call can focus on details and adjustments to make the offer perfect.
However, sales calls are expensive! Otherwise, all marketing would be personal. Careful use of selling time and effective supply of information to select and plan sales calls will influence the effectiveness of the call.

18
A better bottom line

Customizing a brand will bring in more sales and profits unless the costs for the customization process get out of hand. In this chapter we will explore why sales will increase and indicate a few issues relating to operational efficiencies.

MAKING MONEY FROM CUSTOMIZED BRANDING

Profits are necessary for a business to survive. They provide cash for development and a security blanket against future uncertainty. Employees of a profitable company are as a rule much happier and more efficient than those in struggling companies. The level of profit is a tangible piece of evidence of a company's success. Consequently, any marketing concept, and any part of marketing, must be judged against its ability to influence profits positively, in the short and long term.

Marketing costs are sometimes termed investments, which they are. Spending money on advertising, product development or a better customer database is an investment to generate future earnings. Sometimes the return is quick, sometimes it takes time. This can cause problems in companies with a short-term focus as marketing costs almost always are considered in accounting terms to be expenses, not investments.

The financial 'requirement' for immediate return is a problem with many traditional marketing expenses; with customized branding this problem can become much bigger. The reality is that it takes time for investments in the infrastructure to manage a customized brand to pay off. It apparently took Tesco around 3 years to get the benefits of its Clubcard system beyond the initial tactical advantages. Many other schemes we have reviewed have had similar lead times. The reason is simply that it takes time to understand customer data to be able to develop really effective segmentation models and to use the information to provide a better service.

To establish a system to collect data usually takes at least 6 months. It takes another 6 month by a very experienced team to make sense of it all – if the team starts from scratch it will take much longer, maybe 1–4 years. The next phase is to change the way the company is working so that the customization process permeates every part of the customer interface. Not something that is done overnight. From this follow several important conclusions.

1   It is an investment, don't expect a quick fix and don't believe those who promise one, although experience can save months, even years.
2   The key investment is not the computer system or data collection system. The key investment is in brain power, manpower and management to make it happen.
3   It is not necessary to do everything at once. It may be better to take a piecemeal approach and learn by doing. In this way the investment is spread over time and the returns will start to come earlier, although the profits may be smaller.
4   Because it takes time, not all companies are prepared to invest and wait, so those starting out on the road to delivering a customized brand will have less competitive pressure as some competitors will not be prepared to 'play the game'.
5   Because there is a lead time and a learning curve, those at the front of the curve have a competitive window they can exploit to strengthen their market position. A low-price strategy can be copied overnight. A new advertising platform can be created over months. A customized branding strategy takes year(s) to catch up with.

Getting the return on investments in customizing the brand can take time but it will be worth the wait.

WHY MORE SALES?

The rationale for more sales was explained at the beginning of the book. Because the brand proposition will be more relevant, the product more appropriate, the message more appealing, the distribution more convenient and the pricing more attractive, sales will increase.

Increase in sales will come from two strands. First, there will be more sales from existing customers. It is almost always easier to get more sales from existing customers than from new ones, so any marketing strategy has to start with the existing customer category. It is also easier to customize to a customer already known than to do this for one who is not. Second, more sales will come from new customers. The new customers will come because the proposition will be more appropriate and it will be easier to find those customers who will be interested as the profile of each segment will be more distinct. If new customers are not attracted, the strategy will fail, as sooner or later the brand will run out of people to sell to.

Many so-called 'loyalty' schemes, the starting point for several customized branding projects ('we have this scheme, how do we make some use of it?'), are introvert, encouraging existing customers only to buy more. A customized branding strategy has to contain a significant element of growth, using the segmentation models to recruit new customers more cost-effectively than using traditional methods.

More relevant and appropriate products and services sell more – it is no more complicated than that.

WHAT ABOUT THE COST SIDE?

To customize a brand costs money. How much more or how much less depends on the circumstances.

In many industries everything is customized anyway, such as the majority of bigger business-to-business projects, and so a more systematic approach will not increase costs in any significant way.

In other industries with a mass-market tradition the oncost may be noticeable but may not be as big as perhaps initially feared. Production processes can be set up to produce in a customized way, logistics systems can be constructed to keep track of different elements. Nowadays every component required to make a Volvo has an individual sticker so that it can be tracked from the subcontractor all through the manufacturing assembly system. Changing such a system to become more customized will not generate any significant oncosts.

Marketing communication does not have to become more costly, although it may happen. The planning will require more work, but the effectiveness per thousand in the audience will increase, so the net effect of communication effectiveness will in most cases be neutral or an improvement over traditional methods.

Setting up a system to manage customer segmentation can easily be a bottomless pit of IT systems. Expensive data warehouses costing millions of pounds or dollars are unfortunately common, so are expensive CRM systems which are set up to be able to customize a customer interface. According to an article in the *Harvard Business Review*, CRM investments are costing US companies between $60 million and $130 million.

However, it is not necessary with such IT systems to customize a brand. A customer record system set up to track behaviour from a marketing point of view is the only IT investment requirement other than a system to analyse and segment. This assumes of course that the quality of customer data is of a good standard! Otherwise, it is 'rubbish in – rubbish out' that will rule.

The intention here is not to advise on IT and systems solutions but to put across just two points. First, marketing analysis is best done off-line, independent of the main computer system of a company. Second, to do the analysis will in most cases only require the power of a 'normal', high-specification PC. The total customer analysis for all tactical, direct mail campaigns for a big UK bank is run on one PC. That is, the segmentation, the classification and the conclusions all come out of one PC. It is not the ability to do calculations that determines whether a segmentation process will be successful or not. It is the human brains controlling, instructing and interpreting the processing that are important.

These costs must, however, be less than the additional margin generated by extra sales, everything else being equal. If not, cost elements will need to be stripped out of the system, and the company will need to focus on those elements of customizing the brand it can do cost-effectively and where the added value is higher than the added cost.

As in any management process the key to efficiencies is to set up processes that are easy to manage and uncomplicated. To customize the brand does introduce an element of fragmentation across the company which can, if not managed well, lead to cost increases. To run a customized brand does, in other words, put a great focus on the ability to manage. For a well-run company this is a bonus. The fewer companies that can deliver a customized brand, the less competition and the better the market position for those who can.

It will cost some money – but it will be worthwhile.

ANY SAVINGS?

The main focus of customizing the brand is to generate more sales due to a stronger competitive position, which in turn is due to greater relevance for the customer. The cost obviously has to be controlled and be less than the revenue. But, is it possible that a change to what in effect is a more elaborate system can generate any savings?

The answer is a qualified yes, at least on two counts:

1   That a more relevant brand proposition, and in particular the product part, may mean less rejects and waste. By knowing more about the customer and thus producing something that is more appropriate, the risks for something being wrong or going to waste is reduced.
2   That better customer understanding will lead to better forecasting. Knowing more will improve planning and thus reduce inventories. Customizing the product or service also means a

greater element of production on demand, which can remove a lot of costs. Dell computers have saved considerable amounts of money by producing everything to order.

There may be savings – but don't count on it.

CONCLUSIONS

A customized brand will give the customer a higher perceived value leading to increasing sales and/or margin. The costs for delivering a customized brand proposition do not have to increase, but if they do the costs have to be considerably less than the additional gross margin generated. Otherwise the company will have failed in its mission to provide a better offer.

19
What does it take?

Great ideas and great strategies are good ingredients for a successful brand marketing strategy, but a very important one, in my experience, is also the ability to do it, to make it happen. What does a programme to introduce and run a customized brand require from an organizational perspective? This chapter gives some ideas of where to focus.

MANAGEMENT

For a brand to be customized effectively it must be tightly and properly defined, as explained earlier on. The management requirements are similar. The process must be held together tightly to avoid getting out of hand. This can easily happen under normal circumstances; with many more activities going on, the chances of it happening are even greater.

This tight control must however, in our view, be balanced by a will to delegate responsibility as far as possible to get the point of decision as close to the customer interface as is feasible. Actually, the clearer the brand proposition, the easier it is to delegate as all know what is required to deliver a superior brand experience to each customer.

The leading Swedish bank Svenska Handelsbanken has a unique track record in Scandinavian banking in that it is the only bank that has shown consistent profitability over decades. Even in the early 1990s when all other banks in the region had to beg for government help, Svenska managed very well. The bank has a stated management policy of bringing customer responsibility as close as possible to the customer. This means that its customer organization, including marketing, is centred on the branches' responsibility for individual customers, leaving the central units as support functions.

Whether a brand team should be organized per customer segment or not remains an unsettled question. Logically, a customer segment approach has great merit. Each team focuses totally on one part of the market. For a one brand and one product concept company this makes sense and usually works very well. For companies with several brands and concepts it is still theoretically the best approach but in practical terms not always so. Brand management 'has to' override customer segments as brand management is a proactive function, not reactive. For a proactive function to work there needs to be a strong 'heart' pumping out initiatives and ideas. For the heart to work it needs to be in one piece! If customer orientation becomes the overriding structure, the business become reactive, no 'heart' is necessary, just 'arms and legs' to do what it is told to do.

Another element that is of great importance is structure. Structure in particular in the form of information flow. A customized brand business is an information-driven business. It is information about the customers that is influencing and inspiring how to adapt the brand proposition to each segment. From early on the company needs to structure the information flow so that it drives brand consideration before department consideration – 'what is best for the brand' rather than 'what is best for us in department *x*'.

'What is measured is what people will do' is a common slogan with a strong element of truth in it. If customer retention scores are published, people will work on customer retention. If the number of visitors to a store is considered important, people will work on activities generating more visitors. From this it follows that the key indicators of success need to be chosen with great care, taking into particular consideration brand management objectives.

When it comes to frequency of information flow, technically most customer information can be distributed on a daily basis but in most cases that is an unnecessary sophistication. Even though one bank may change its customized mailing programme on the basis of what happened up until the day before the mailing, in most cases, and probably also in the case of this particular bank, that adds very little to its effectiveness but it can add extra costs. In most cases customer behaviour does not change very much over the shorter term. Up-to-date, nanosecond-driven information almost always costs more than it adds in commercial effectiveness. After all, lifestyle attitudes and life stage information hardly change over night.

The companies that are closest to a customized brand model don't process information, they publish the information. The brand data analysis team does not supply data on spreadsheets, they supply information in easy to follow charts. An executive treats a report that is to be published differently to a report that is written. This is a way of thinking that can influence how customer information is used in the daily work by executives at different levels.

In essence managing a customized brand marketing function is no different from any brand marketing group – just a bit more difficult. Difficulty is a challenge and a route to competitive advantage.

Establish a structure for managing the customization process – otherwise it may go off the rails.

FEEDBACK

All companies need feedback and all executives in a company need feedback, yet so often, so little attention is given to proper systems to provide this information.

A customized brand business is information-driven, as stated earlier. It is thus in such an environment that it is relatively easy to build in feedback loops in almost all respects. Answers can be given to questions like: What happened to customer loyalty after marketing campaign X or product initiative Y? Did size of purchase increase after Z was changed? Has the new sales executive in region Y changed customer behaviour? What kind of customers were generated in the latest new business campaign?, etc.

For many, feedback is seen to be 'boring'. Publish instead of send and it is less boring. If still boring, consider whether the individuals actually understand the information. If still boring, consider whether the person(s) actually is interested in and suitable to be working in a customized brand environment.

Feedback is essential. It is a great learning tool. With proper feedback systems mistakes can be forgiven because the organization has learnt something. Without feedback, and therefore not learning, the mistake is a waste. With feedback the mistake may actually be a very useful investment in customer understanding.

Where most companies fail is in documenting the feedback, building the corporate memory on paper (or digitally). In particular where staff turnover is high, to document whatever is learnt is very important for obvious reasons – otherwise you only teach the individual, not the organization. And then when the individual leaves, the company has in effect contributed to another organization's learning rather than its own. So, establish simple and easy to follow routines for documenting the results of the feedback loops.

Without feedback there is no learning – with documented feedback there is learning, development and progress.

FIND A PREACHER

Almost any new concept requires an internal champion. In each successful case we have studied or been involved in whether in retailing, banking or any other sector, there has been a champion at a senior level, pushing the concept forward among senior colleagues as well as among his or her own staff.

This is not unique to this concept. In many companies, where the task is still to instil some sort of marketing thinking, the concept of customizing the brand is far from the current agenda. But that is no reason for complacency.

The task to preach constantly is sometimes rather thankless but part and parcel of the role of senior marketing executives. It just has to be done if success is to be achieved. It is so easy to fall back into old ways of doing things, to lower expectations and be satisfied with 'OK' rather than 'great'. Constant reminders, packed in different words and themes, plus high-profile announcements of success are ways to convert people and ensure they stay on the right track.

Preach every day to everyone you meet.

CONCLUSIONS

One word not mentioned above is 'guts'. It takes guts to achieve something new, to take the risk of changing the way the brand has been managed. If no guts and no change, the brand will be playing in the second division very soon, rather than in the premier league. What it takes to succeed is common sense, understanding of brands, consistency and persistence. The rest, the how to do it, can always be picked up along the way.

20
Conclusions and summary

SUMMARIZING

The purpose of this book is to explain the concept of customized branding and the brand marketing and business advantages it offers. The rationale is that a customized brand is a stronger brand. So, what is a strong brand? A strong brand is one that:

a is top of mind and is number one in the category – first choice;
b outperforms competition in the minds of the customers – so customers stay;
c outperforms competition in the minds of the public – so new customers will come and existing ones will feel comfortable about staying;
d is differentiated to competition – no brand confusion and a distinct reason for being chosen; and
e makes money for the company and makes staff proud.

A customized brand will fulfil these requirements because it will be more relevant, more appealing and better tailored to the needs of the individual than mass-market average brands.

From a customized brand point of view, this book falls into the self-selection category. A wide range from which the reader can self-select the most important ideas. The choice will differ depending on circumstances such as company position, market sector, experience and personal interests.

As the brand owner of this book I have below outlined what I consider to be the 21 main points of the book, one for each chapter, the preface and introduction included. The reader may not agree but I hope most will ring true and serve as reminders of the contents. The 21 key points:

Preface	Average brands are no fun, and will not remain profitable.
Introduction	We are all individuals and like to be treated that way.
1	A customized brand is one that delivers to each customer an individualized, differentiated brand proposition and a brand experience that is totally relevant.
2	History proves that a customized brand is always preferred – if it can be sold at a price that is acceptable in comparison with a mass-marketed brand.
3	To customize the brand proposition is the ultimate step on the ladder to total relevance and differentiation, and it is at least as important in business to business as in consumer marketing.
4	More and more of everything means better opportunities for customizing the brand.
5	Segmentation is the key tool to understanding customers and to be able to deliver a customized brand proposition.
6	Finding the Big Number will make the customization process easier and more powerful.
7	Developing and managing the ten steps to a customized brand is a dynamic process full of grey shades.
8	There is, though, no point starting unless the competition and the category is properly defined.
9	Use customer data to find and to be able to focus on the best customers, those who spend the most.
10	Define the brand with care, and with it what the company is really good at.
11	Adapt the brand proposition to each customer segment while maintaining the sense of a totality.

12   Use customer information to build a better mousetrap and then make different versions for each segment.

13   Make sure all customers can get the product and do consider several different channels to market.

14   Differentiated pricing is the right model but in a way which makes sense to all customer segments.

15   Individualize and segment marketing communication but make sure the brief is in place first.

16   To include a sales promotion element in the first stage of a brand customization process is not a bad idea.

17   Don't ignore the ultimate customized brand vehicle, the personal sales call.

18   A customized brand will make more money for the company but it may take time. On the other hand, if not customized, the brand may not survive.

19   For management the watchwords are structure and feedback.

CONCLUSION – ONE DAY ALL MARKETING WILL BE LIKE THIS

Marketing as practised has not in the vast majority of cases taken advantage of the explosion in the possibilities to collect and use customer data to drive brands forward. There is a great opportunity to be had in using data to get closer to the customer, to be able to provide a better service or supply a better product and thus gain higher sales and more loyal customers. Marketing can now move into a phase of contributing in a much stronger way to the success of companies.

Customized branding is already happening in bits and pieces in many companies. By developing a structured and proactive strategy, this piecemeal approach can be turned into a dynamo for developing brands, businesses and markets. The brands and companies that don't will be left in the dark and disappear, surrendering their market positions.

WHAT TO DO TOMORROW, AND THE DAY AFTER ...

As tomorrow is the first day of the rest of the life of the brand, here are some suggestions on what to do:

1 Check what customer data is available, structure it and start to collect what may be missing.
2 Review the brand platform and define any missing parts.
3 Document what elements of the marketing mix are already customized.
4 Start building a segmentation model.
5 Define what to do to make the current customization activities more brand-driven.
6 Build a programme for developing customized brand propositions.

Index